FAR FOREIGN LAND

LAND

Tony Evans

YWWA
Tony

AB PUBLISHING

British Library Cataloguing in Publication Data
A record for this book is available from
the British Library

ISBN 978-0-9558727-0-9

Cover design: Ian Richardson Photo Alex Benwell

For Alisa,
who has given me love,
inspiration and the gift of Grace
And Grace, who sings the songs I sang

Acknowledgements

THERE ARE MANY people I would like to thank, too many to list. My family have been crucial, helping me find the right track on the many times I have lost my way on the journey. Margaret, my mother, John, Julie and Stephen, my brothers and sister, deserve much credit. My cousins, Joan, Terry and Kevin, have also given me great support.

In particular, I would like to mention Annie and Minnie, my aunts, whose gift of a word processor that they could barely afford resurrected a stalled writing career.

Naomi Roth has been central to the development of this book and I am grateful for her patience and invaluable advice.

Special thanks to Juliana Pereira, whose contribution was vital to this second edition. Praise, too should go to Dave Ramsbottom who, as a Preston fan, knows how important history is in the game. I'm grateful to Joachim von Halasz, too, and Kelly Parker and Sean Mumbray at thirtyninezero.

And finally, thanks to all the friends who rode the trains across Britain and Europe with me over the years. Most are mentioned in the following pages. See you at the match.

Contents

Foreword

THIS SHORT BOOK is the result of an unforgettable few months in 2005 and a series of unlikely events that seemed to take on a momentum of their own. On the first Monday in January, I began a new job as Deputy Football Editor at *The Times*, having been promoted to the position by Tim Hallissey, the new Sports Editor. That was enough to make my year. Where the journey would take me after that, I could not imagine.

Against all expectation, Liverpool, the club I was born to support, went on a run to the Champions League final. Twenty years earlier, at another final in Brussels, a dreadful 12 months ended with the deaths of 39 innocent people. This disaster was brought to the forefront of our minds when we drew Juventus, the team whose fans had died at Heysel, in the quarter-finals.

This is the story of eight days in May, after Tim had the brilliant idea of setting me loose to take the train from one end of Europe to the other to get to the final in Istanbul. Of course, to explain the significance of those eight days I have to step outside this short trip. It became a journey to some dark places – both metaphorically and literally. As the spring wore on, I realised that my experiences of the mid-1980s were so tied in with the run to Istanbul that the story could only be made complete by retelling the entire tale.

Much has changed in the time between the two finals. In 1985, though we could not imagine it, football was about to be transformed. The derided and vulgar sport was on the cusp of becoming shiny, globalised entertainment. The game that started in churches and work can-

7

teens was about to embark on a money-driven journey – given extra impetus by two mind-boggling disasters – that would place it, in 2005, as the cash-cow of choice for American carpetbaggers and Russian oligarchs.

Amazingly, glory has become less important in football in this time. Finishing fourth in a league – or even seventeenth – has come to be considered move valuable than winning trophies. One night in Istanbul nailed that lie. This is how I got there.

Foreword to the second edition

Much has happened in the three years since I wrote this book. It is clear now that Istanbul was a turning point in the globalisation of the game. Liverpool Football Club now has foreign ownership and supporters have been forced to become more proactive in maintaining their sense of culture. Their efforts - Keep Flags Scouse, Reclaim The Kop and, most recently, Sons of Shankly, the supporters' union - have not met with everyone's approval but they represent the best chance of keeping something of the game "ours" instead of letting it slip into the hands of the money-men.

I have been pleased to find so many people - especially among the younger supporters - hold similar views to mine. We will not be forced away from the game without a battle.

I have made no changes, except to correct some factual mistakes, because the point of the book was as much to provide a snapshot of a moment as anything else. If it feels like ancient history, the emotions that drive it are still very much alive...
Tony Evans
March 2008

PART ONE

1

I will tell you the story
of a poor boy

A TEXT MESSAGE CAME through just after the half-time whistle blew. 'God's good,' it said. It was not meant as consolation. It was gloating. Across the Liverpool section in the stadium, people sat in silence, with a bemused, helpless look on their faces. It was cold and most seemed to be squirming in their seats. If there was anywhere to go to get warmth and comfort, most would surely head in that direction.

Not far away, a man stood up and, with a voice filled with pure spite, started to sing.

> 'When you walk
> Through a storm,
> Hold your head up high…'

And, after a slow start, when it looked as if the song would stall and not take hold, more and more people hauled themselves to their feet and joined in. Well, we might be beaten, we might be a long way from home, we might be supporting a heartless bunch of losers, but at least we could show the Italians and anyone watching on television that mere defeat can't break our spirit.

So, we rose and sang, putting every ounce of our beings into it, and that hackneyed, cliched, plodding song became soul music, like it does every once in a while. A perverse miracle of emotional chemistry was underway with the mix of despair, anger and defiance somehow emerging as uplifting pride. This song gains eloquence and potency in defeat and, tonight, it was a philosophical circling of the wagons. It articulated a dry-eyed resistance and commitment. We stood unbowed, even though rout and humiliation were invevitable.

Liverpool were only losing 3-0 in the European Cup final, so it wasn't a weeping matter. Worse things happen. We know.

When the song finished, someone chanted: 'Four-three, we're going to win four-three...' And we laughed, really hard, before joining in. After the passion we'd just emitted, there was a need for light relief. The next 45 minutes were not going to be pleasant. Relax, don't take it seriously. It's only football. It's not a matter of life or death...

More than an hour later, after midnight in a Turkish field miles from civilisation, a man upsides of 17st leapt upon me and kissed me hard. It was not a nightmare filched from *Midnight Express*, but one of the greatest moments anyone could experience. 'How did it happen?' he asked as I staggered backwards and fought off a hernia. 'How the hell did we get here?'

The simple answer was by train. From Lime Street to Istanbul over four surreal days. He didn't mean that. The journey he was talking about was more metaphysical, taking 20 years, from youth to middle age. Or he may have meant... but it's easier to talk about rolling stock, timetables and the long ride from Anfield to Ataturk.

How many journeys have started and finished with a pint in the Yankee? Too many to recall. This bar holds an iconic place in the folklore of a certain type of Liverpool supporter, the tales of mad nights there exaggerated and cherished across generations.

More than 20 years ago, when long, glorious hauls across Europe were the rule rather than the exception, the Yankee was in full flight.

Some argue that it was the birthplace of naked pole dancing – even if girls rarely ventured in on deranged Saturday nights.

Some considered it admirable to climb the support column in the middle of the bar area and, on wilder nights, young scallies would shin up to the ceiling and lead the chanting from on high. Because they were full of ale and likely to drop on to the clientele and cause a disturbance, the management greased the pole to make this sport more difficult. The slippy, sticky stuff wasn't a deterrent in itself – it added an extra dimension to the triumph of successful climbers – but the effect it had on Lacostes and diamond Pringle sweaters led to complaints and a drop off in takers for the challenge. That was until an enterprising and well-dressed youth stripped to his boxers and showed how it should be done. And if the young buck drunk enough or stupid enough to fancy a date with the pole was wearing designer underwear, off came the skiddies. The Yankee was that sort of place.

In this bar, preconceptions about Liverpool, the city, are often reaffirmed and subverted in single acts. At one time, under former ownership, a home-made poster adorned the dingy back-room area. It had a photograph of a large group of young men and, underneath, the legend: 'The Yankee Bar on tour. As seen on *Crimewatch*.' Dotted around the periphery of the montage were clumsily-snipped cutouts of desirable consumer goods: a watch, a fridge, a television, a video recorder... Irony or a glorification of criminality? A bit of both.

It was almost empty at 7.30 on Thursday May 19, a full six days before the European Cup final. A sign over the bar said: 'In the interests of health and safety, please keep your shoes on.' Only three people were drinking and they appeared fully shod.

If you're going to set out for a trip to Istanbul for a big match, this is the place to start. More than Anfield, more than the Cavern, this is the heart of the city for some of us. Here, the mythology of Liverpool away travel has been embellished and sung about - and events that never even happened happily remembered.

Pubs close to railway stations often draw the rootless, the unstable, the dangerous and the plainly mad. There are plenty like that always hanging around in the Yankee, giving it the atmosphere of a frontier bar. It always feels like you are going abroad from here, because when you're Scouse abroad is pretty close. Even Halewood and Huyton seem like colonised areas about to slip out of the city's grasp, with the Lancashire accent and people creeping back in. You hit alien land before you hit the Runcorn Bridge and once across the Mersey you're deep in a different country - England.

But don't go and try to find the Yankee. That is not the bar's official name. Taking Scouse voices at face value can be confusing for outsiders. Like the Flat Iron, another favoured drinking place of the extremist wing of Liverpool fans, the Yankee will not be located by a pub sign. Conversely, ask for these places by their real names and even some of the locals will be confused. Anyway, it's a place to start a journey, not a destination. A last pint there and the adventure begins.

* * *

Even in the age of easyJet, the train is still – at least in the football fan's imagination – the classic mode of travel. The whole concept of large numbers of away fans started in the 1950s when young men began to have enough disposable income to make journeys across the country to watch matches.

Liverpool and Everton led the way, the exuberant and sometimes unacceptable behaviour of the fans earning them the tag 'Mersey maniacs'. Travelling support was born at Lime Street.

Even for trips abroad, the train has its legends. Foremost is the excursion to Rome in 1977 for the European Cup final against Borussia Monchengladbach. The special trains left Liverpool on Monday morning, dropped their passengers for less than 12 hours in Rome for the match, and arrived back at Lime Street in the early hours of Saturday morning. No food and water were provided in the carriages but those who made this dreadful journey have heroic status in the annals of Kopite legend. One middle-aged supporter said that he'd been captured by the Germans at Anzio in 1944 and conditions leaving Italy were considerably worse in 1977. He did, however, note that it felt better this time: at least the Germans had been beaten and he was going home.

When the trains from Rome arrived at Lime Street all those years ago, the passengers hung out of the windows waving chequered flags acquired in Italy and sang joyfully. To hear them, it had been a relaxing trip back. Closer inspection told a different tale. A large number of travellers had chosen to wear white flared trousers to complement the obligatory red shirt. This unisex legwear invariably proved unrealistic for the short hop to Wembley. For the long haul to Italy, with the toilets blocked and coughing up their contents into the carriages early in the journey, they were an outright mistake. The sound of chanting arrived at the waiting crowds only slightly ahead of the odour. So this was the smell of victory.

There was no buffet car on those trains to Rome and no water available for 24 hours on the way back as the carriages sat in a siding in Switzerland for an entire day with unexplained problems.

The train my mother and younger brother were on limped back into Liverpool after 2am on Saturday and, by then, the nightclubs had disgorged and there were no taxis to be found in the city centre. Grubby and exhausted, most of those who had got off the train faced a long walk home. It was the final trial of an epic journey.

Some of us had no sympathy. Tales of filth, hunger and thirst only generated envy. Those of us who had been left behind to watch the match on television harboured deep resentments.

In the 1980s, Alexei Sayle wrote a novel based on this trip called *Train to Hell*. In it, he described Liverpool as 'Beirut with job centres'. By May 2005, the unemployment rates of two decades earlier had fallen considerably and the botched facelift of superficial regeneration gives the impression that all is well – at least in the centre. But Merseyside is not a

rich area. The cost of getting to Istanbul caused considerable grief and
tore families apart. Fathers were separated from their children – they
couldn't afford to take the kids to Turkey – causing rifts that may never
be healed. In 20 years' time, bitter middle-aged men will be telling their
children: 'No I wasn't there. Him, your Granddad, didn't take me.
Because of money.'

In 1977, the excuse to leave me at home was different. Exams were
used to justify the decision. Now, it seems inconceivable that anyone
could believe that a commerce 'O' level was a fair trade-off for
Liverpool's first European Cup final. In truth, the reasons were probably
commercial at heart. There was just not enough cash to get three people
in our family to Rome. It took a visit to the pawnshop to get two on that
train.

It is different these days. Credit cards have changed everything. And
because of this, the autumn of 2005 will long be remembered by debt-
collecting firms as 'the great Liverpool boom'. Those who could got to
Istanbul by any means possible and raised the money any way they
could manage. In early May, a psychotic episode was under way on the
Lancashire bank of the Mersey. Flight prices were unreasonably high,
hotel accommodation nearly impossible to attain but the desperation to
get to the game was palpable. This was not just any old match. So many
conflicting emotions and memories had been exposed by the route to
the final that it felt like a sort of redemption – as if a form of healing
beckoned.

Mulling all this over, it was time to finish the pint, take a last look at
the Yankee and go and take a seat on the train to Euston to begin the
long trip across Europe.

2

They all laugh at us, they all mock us

I T HAD NOT BEEN a good start. To go 1-0 down so early was a shock. But the worst moment of the night came after 39 minutes. Alessandro Nesta, turned by Luis Garcia for once, slipped and, seeing he was beaten, the Milan defender knocked the ball away with his arm. Penalty. I was right on line and saw Nesta's shift of the shoulder and guilty, surprised look when the referee played on. I was still frozen, pointing to the position of the foul, when Hernan Crespo made it 2-0 at the other end.

The sound of the crowd when the opposition scores is strange. It is disembodied, as if played back through a static-ridden radio. It does not interfere with the shock and silence around you. There, in this cocoon of stunned disappointment, I continued standing in the same position for a full minute, arm aimed at the spot of Nesta's offence like a linesman who had suffered a stroke, repeating: 'Penalty, penalty, penalty,' in increasingly hysterical tones. Then, an even more depressing thought struck: Crespo, on loan at Milan, was still a Chelsea player. How would you like that raw wound, Sir? With salt on it?

* * *

As a city, Liverpool has placed too much of its identity in its football teams. Individuals, too. For the first part of the trip, alone until Vienna, there was plenty of time to reflect on this. I remember reading *Fever Pitch*, Nick Hornby's book, where he talks about the first match he attended, how he came in from the back of the terraces and saw the crowd and the pitch and was captivated. 'Entryist,' I snarled and threw the book down. It is perhaps an exaggeration – but only slight – but I always claim I knew I was a Liverpool fan before I knew my name. First game? No idea. Too young.

It is impossible to imagine football not being part of your life. There are people who contend that the state of obsession that many of us exist with is an affectation, a lifestyle choice. It's not. Right from the beginning, from the first moment that my consciousness registered as a memory, I've known that it is part of my being. And it can skew the way you look at life.

It was once suggested to a friend, whose marriage was sliding downhill, that perhaps it would be prudent if he put some of the time, money and effort spent attending away games into his relationship. 'I had Liverpool before I knew her,' he said. 'And when I no longer know her, they'll still be there.'

Some women take this attitude as a challenge and believe that they can turn you – straighten you out. They can only lose in an unequal battle. I've known men whose heads have been turned by girlfriends, fans who have carped at the expense of travel and tickets in a strangely robotic, unconvincing voice and taken up more acceptable pursuits at weekends that involve their new love. But sooner or later the sight of men in shorts will stir their emotions. The stroking of a ball 40 yards into space for a man to run on to will set their pulses racing out of control and they will be pulled back towards their natural bent.

Back in the 1980s, we were discussing a friend who had not turned up at Lime Street for an away trip.

'What's he doing today?'

'He's taking a girl out,' the answer came, dripping with scorn.

'What a queer,' someone said.

The football teams in Liverpool filled a huge cultural void in a city that was uncertain about its identity for much of the twentieth century. Many citizens are ambivalent about England, a zeitgeist captured in the 1960s by Johnny Speight, who had Alf Garnett rebuke Mike, his son-in-law, for being a 'traitorious Scouse git'. In a town that has such an Irish heritage and similar – but milder – religious divisions to Belfast and Glasgow, there's not much of a sense of Englishness.

And it works both ways. You don't exactly get the warmest of welcomes in the rest of England. Scousers are labelled thieves and considered workshy and militant. And the accent seems to short-circuit some people's brains. In the late 1990s I worked for Chelsea when the ground was undergoing extensive renovations. Leaving Stamford Bridge on a winter afternoon, I hailed a taxi. 'You're a long way from home, Scouse,' the driver said. It was a rebuke. The conversation continued: 'What are you doing at the Bridge? Not a Chelsea fan, surely?'

'No, work there.'

'I don't envy you on the building in this weather. What are you, a brickie?'

I was wearing a Versace suit. He just didn't see it. The accent vibrated on his eardrums and immediately scrambled all his other senses. He took an unfeasibly long time examining the £20 note I offered before handing me any change. No tip there, then.

The journey to Istanbul took me back to Chelsea. They were the opponents in the semi-final and although the London club are the epitome of nouveau riche – bags of Russian money but only two titles in 100 years – they expected Liverpool to doff a cap and provide a red carpet on their way to Turkey. The bitterness and rage when we didn't play their game was palpable… Thieving Scouse gits indeed. Chelsea and their fans learnt a harsh lesson over the two legs: you can sell your soul, but even all those roubles can't buy divine right.

The trip from Lime Street to London is very familiar. Aside from the away matches, so many of us have taken the route to find employment. There's a moment of epiphany that marks the end of childhood: Napoleon said it was when he realised he would die; for those of us who grew up in Liverpool in the 70s and 80s, it was when we understood that we would have to leave home and family to find work. The ticket to Euston was predestined for many of us.

Yet London has fine memories. The first landmark on the journey from Lime Street to Istanbul was unfamiliar – the new Wembley arch. Back in 1978, Liverpool won the European Cup under the old twin towers, beating Bruges 1-0. The team was so good and the performance so disappointing that many of us didn't realise what an achievement it was.

The game has changed since 1978. Then, Chelsea had no money, players with names like Ray, Tommy and Micky and fans with names like, well, Ray, Tommy and Micky. Stamford Bridge was a hostile place to go. More than any club, Chelsea illustrate how football has developed and how it has moved away from its traditional constituency.

By the Champions League semi-final of 2005, Chelsea had acquired a billionaire owner in Roman Abramovich. The club had spent big on players with names like Claude, Ricardo and Didier and were cheered on by fans with names like Giles.

In London for the first leg of the semi-final, the crowd were quite restrained – apart from in the Liverpool section. It's hard to imagine how Stamford Bridge was granted a safety certificate. The entrance to the away section was under the main stand in April 2005, effectively creating a subway area that can be entered without a ticket. Into this confined space came hundreds of Liverpool fans intent on seeing the match but lacking the precious rectangle of paper that would set the turnstile clicking. So, as the police lost control, the gates were stormed. It was every man for himself and plenty of people were crushed. Although it was a minor case of push and shove, the potential for a serious incident was clear.

Inside, the stands of the Taylor Report were turned into terraces with more people crammed in than could be seated. The plastic back supports of the seats became shin-high tripwires as spectators at the rear craned forward to see, pushing down on the backs of those in front. No one, least of all the Liverpool supporters, had learnt the lessons of the past. The desire to see the game over-rode all other considerations for some.

The emotional intensity of the away fans that night passed largely unnoticed as the press wondered why Giles and the chaps hadn't managed the right level of rah-rah to disturb the unwashed northerners during the 0-0 draw. Two weeks later, that craving – 'the dense and the driven passion' – came to the fore as Anfield exhibited a collective will that seemed to transmit itself to the players on a night that entered football legend. The ferocity of purpose from the stands communicated itself to the players and even created the illusion that Chelsea had conceded a goal. The fourth-minute winner will be debated for years as no one can say for certain whether Luis Garcia's shot was blocked by William Gallas before it entered the net but the goal was given anyway and Liverpool were on their way to Istanbul. I hope it never crossed the line.

The anguish in west London was tangible. It was their cup, they thought. They forgot to remember that we had already won it four times, in the days when you could only enter as a result of real achievement – either winning the domestic title or defending the trophy. And the Wembley arch brought thoughts of our successful defence of the European Cup in 1978.

Graeme Souness angled a ball through the Bruges defence, Kenny Dalglish chipped over the goalkeeper and the big cup stayed in the Anfield trophy cabinet. I was up at the opposite end, the Bruges end - no ticket that day, either; some things never change - and only the silence told me that we'd scored. I'd picked the previous night to get paralytic for the first time (on rum and black, for God's sake) and was still in need of hospital treatment and unable to focus when Dalglish struck.

That was two European Cups by 1978. At that time, no Chelsea supporter could have imagined that their team would ever be within a game of playing for the trophy. They might even have struggled to believe their team would win the League, having only won it once, in 1955. Fifty years on, they won their second title but seemed to take little joy in it after the defeat by Liverpool. Around the Kings Road, they seemed to resent being knocked out by a 'smaller' club.

Where did they get such an inflated idea about their status? The ability to outbid any other club in the planet is part of it but there is also a wider issue. When the money-grubbers at Uefa diluted the competition for the European Cup by allowing as many as four sides from a single country to play in the Champions League, it let teams like Chelsea compete with the Continent's best without having any real record of success. You can finish runners-up, third or even fourth in the league and live under the illusion that it is acceptable to mention the club in the same breath as Real Madrid, AC Milan and Liverpool, whose trophy cabinets are brimming with domestic titles as well as European Cups.

At Stamford Bridge, their memory is about as extensive as their achievements. Arrogance so often comes without self-awareness and, when you reinvent yourself, it is easy to pretend the past did not happen. Huge spending power does not automatically turn a club into the biggest in the world. There is still a different sort of accounting in football – and Chelsea need much more silverware in the bank to support their delusions of grandeur.

3

Sent him off to a far foreign land

EVEN WHEN THERE'S NO hope, you have to fight back. Resistance is an end in itself. So, as soon as the players came back on the pitch, there was plenty of fist-clenching and a gritted-teeth hubbub. Just get one, they're Italians, they're mentally weak… Sometimes, the only fallback position is placing your hope in tanks-with-reverse-gears clichés.

Football makes nonsense of relativity. Time accelerates and decelerates over the course of 90 minutes so that even with a watch and a scoreboard clock it's hard to keep tabs on where you are. It felt like half an hour had passed since half-time when John Arne Riise finally managed to get his cross in after a failed first attempt. Stevie Gerrard rose to the ball and, so it appeared, flicked it in. Nine minutes had passed in the half.

We couldn't see, from our angle, the power he'd put into it. He couldn't know the power he'd unleashed.

Consolation goal celebrations are different. You don't hug strangers and you pull the air-punch. It's another deep breath and an imploring, low-register grunt of 'come on'. Gerrard didn't seem to think we were excited enough. He made lifting gestures straight across to the area where we were standing, as if he was angry at us. We were still angry at him.

'I don't need lessons in supporting from you,' I howled.

The first part of the journey didn't really feel like an away trip. Train travel usually happens in the company of a group of other fans and the time is whiled away with a mixture of banter and boredom but there was little to do now but reflect on the wider journey. From London, the Eurostar took me to the Gare du Nord in Paris. I didn't recognise it.

The last time I came off a train here on the way to a European Cup final, in 1981, a man who disembarked in front of me was wearing a flag that said 'Paris on the dole'. There were plenty of similar banners – songs, too.

'On the dole,
drinking wine,
Gay Paree…'

You couldn't help but feel proud. In many ways it was better than winning the cup - being able to give a collective two-fingered salute to the Thatcher Government and show them that we had the enterprise to get on our bikes. The rest of the country would tune into the match on television and see our message to them.

What was that message? I don't think we were sure. Maybe that despite all the economic, political and social pressure that the city was under in the early 1980s, we were unconquered. Clearly, many of us who travelled to that European Cup final in Paris were out of step with mainstream Britain. We moved increasingly left, confusing Thatcherism with Conservatism and failed to realise that the Government was more radical and more intent on changing the face of the nation than the Militant Tendency.

A wave of redundancies was passing over the city. We had no jobs, no respect, no power. What we did have was the energy to fight back. And the best football team in the world.

When we sang:
'They all laugh at us, they all mock us,
They all say our days are numbered,
But I was born to be Scouse,

Victorious are we...' it wasn't just about football.

So 11 men in red shirts dominating not only England but Europe became a focus for our hopes. Even those who didn't comprehend our thought processes and pride could understand when the word 'Liverpool' sat at the top of a table or a man wearing a Liver Bird on his chest picked up a silver trophy. By God, we were pleased the buggers envied us something.

There was an anger in those songs about being on the dole and a warning on the banners but it was not heeded. Little more than five weeks after Phil Thompson lifted the European Cup in the Parc des Princes, the fury erupted in the area Scousers call Liverpool 8 and the rest of the world would soon know as Toxteth. The riots have been portrayed as having racial undertones, having taken place in the south end of the city, where the black community are congregated. However, the problems were much wider and trouble in the north end was under-reported. Near Anfield itself, the huge block of tenements called Sir Thomas White Gardens saw sporadic rioting. The social and economic problems – and the behaviour of the police in working-class areas in crudely executing the stop and search 'suss' laws – had created a sense of alienation that was widespread across the poorer population.

So we were hardly surprised to find the French police were heavy-handed, too. For the best part of 25 years it had not been romance that came to mind when I heard the phrase 'Paris in the spring'. It was tear gas. The CRS, the French riot police, were waiting for us in 1981 and their previous experience of fans from across the Channel was six years earlier, when Leeds United supporters brought a bit of darkness to the City of Light, rioting in defeat

The CRS were primed when, on a damp spring morning, ticketless Liverpool fans gathered outside the Parc des Princes. The middle-aged, families and the more restrained young men – me among them – formed an orderly queue where a gendarme indicated that there might be tickets available. The wilder elements went looking for touts – and they were neither equipped nor inclined to pay the exorbitant prices demanded by locals.

For some reason, the law in France appears to protect touts. Our boys gave them a friendly buffeting, relieved them of their booty and were rather put out when the CRS intervened with a baton charge. This was good entertainment for our queue and a very acceptable way of passing the time before they sold us some tickets, even if there was much comment that the busies should have been out stopping crime rather than rescuing vile parasites from good-hearted boys who were liberating a few tickets.

Then, as if they'd heard the criticism under their helmets, the CRS turned to face us. They began walking forward. Being positioned conveniently near a bridge over the *Périphérique*, I began to back off. My mate said: 'They won't charge, it's mainly women and kids.' They charged.

It was a situation many football supporters have experienced abroad yet the general population at home will always instinctively side with a police force and assume that any brutality is a result of hooliganism. Here, the scallies had scuttled off, so the CRS assuaged their need to impose themselves by cracking the heads of those least likely to fight back. They wanted to let *Les Rosbifs* know that they were not prepared to have us act like Leeds in 1975.

As we fled across the bridge – the odd bottle-flinger giving us the chance to embellish the tale into a legend of fighting retreat – a tear-gas canister arced overhead.

'Jesus, the bastards are gassing us,' someone said. It was incredible. The French savages had over-reacted. It was almost enough to make you feel good about the Liverpool constabulary. Little did we know that within six weeks the police would be firing CS gas on the streets of Liverpool – the first time such a weapon was used by the authorities on mainland Britain.

Actually, the CRS did us a favour. We staggered through a multi-storey car park and emerged into a street lined with Spanish coaches. Two men were fighting in the middle of the road, but it seemed to have little to do with football. *Madrileños* and Scousers were watching together and seemed friendly enough.

The sight of us weeping brought amusement all round. 'Why are youse crying, boys, haven't you got tickets?' a man said.

We shook our heads. 'Well he's got some.' He pointed to a Real Madrid fan, who beckoned us over.

'How much?' The man pointed to the price on the tickets: 100 francs. We couldn't believe it. Face value. We had just enough money to buy them. Foolishly, we'd spent the majority of our cash drinking in Dover and on the boat to Calais. We were now cleared out, but getting in. And we'd get a drink anyway, because the place was awash with looted wine. We swigged from bottles with Spaniards and told them that their little club could not compete with our side. The older Real fans laughed at us, but we were young and the only history we cared about was our own.

I winced at the memory. The Spaniards must have looked at me like I look at young, mouthy Chelsea fans. Better to think of Alan Kennedy getting into an odd position in the Real penalty area and shooting when the entire Liverpool section were screaming: 'Cross!' His single goal was enough and we took the long journey home happy. It was a hat-trick of European Cups and I recall laughing about the gas on the way home. 'The bastards can gas us every year if we win it,' I said. It was a sentiment remembered with bitterness three years later.

Still, Paris has a different atmosphere without the gas, the rain and the hairy-arsed policemen desperate to put another notch on their baton. You never really experience a city when you visit it as a fan and the City of Light, surprisingly, is quite a nice place on a warm May afternoon.

Some things don't change though, I thought, as I sat outside a café, enjoying the sun and a glass of beer in the short 90 minutes between trains. I was still travelling across Europe without a ticket for a European Cup final. The next stop would be Vienna, where I would be joined by Dave. Frankly, he was the last person I wanted to see. There was something I hated about Dave. He had a ticket.

4

They all say our days are numbered

S O IT WAS OVER. All this way and that was that. Then Crespo struck again. It was too much to bear. The happy Milan fans celebrating at the far end didn't bother me. It was the thought of Mancunians popping champagne, Evertonians dancing in the streets and Chelsea supporters crowing because Crespo had scored twice. They would act like they had won the cup by default. It was bleak, it really was. Football can be such a cruel game.

Finding myself on the old Orient Express between Paris and Vienna felt as unlikely an event as Liverpool reaching the final. There was a veneer of dust on the sleeper carriage but it was easy to evoke the glamour of the past in this mobile, down-on-its-luck hotel. A spectre of elegance still lurked in the first-class carriage.

Before the bed was put down, there were three individual armchairs and a table – plenty of room to relax. The attendant brought a selection of Austrian meats and cheeses, sekt and beer. This was a level of comfort that train-riding football fans can only dream about. And a bed made a change from curling up on the floor or the overhead luggage racks.

Yet there was a glamour in our past, too, even if the last time we went to a European Cup final, 20 years earlier, the mood was very different among Liverpool supporters.

In the face-painting, prawn-sandwich munching, glossy days of the Premiership, it is hard to imagine how football sat in the popular imagination in the mid-1980s. Supporters were demonised in the media and it was almost a matter of shame for the middle classes to admit to an affinity with the game. It was a world where many in the general public lauded Ken Bates, the Chelsea chairman, when he announced plans to erect electrified fences around the playing area to keep supporters penned in. There was a madness afoot in the game and it was not restricted to the clashes between fans that overshadowed the sport.

There was violence at matches; that is undeniable. However, fewer punches were thrown, fewer kicks landed, than the public at large believed. But things had gone too far to rectify. The suggestion of violence, the perceived threat of confrontation, coloured the entire atmosphere around football.

Getting up early on a Saturday morning, boarding a train to another city and being met by hundreds of police at the other end made you feel like you were committing a criminal act. It was fantastic. The excitement was thrilling. Mundane lives were given a lift by a feeling of wildness on Saturdays. That it was mostly bluster did not matter.

There was a huge impression of trouble. Before and after matches, it felt like pitched battles were taking place across the country. Hundreds of youths would charge up streets, hundreds of other youths would scatter, run away, regroup and counter-charge. Scores of police would chase in all directions. A handful of punches were landed.

For the most part, these 'pitched battles' were huge street ballets, given immediacy by a soundtrack of chants and sirens. And it worked for everyone to give them a significance that they did not deserve.

The dumb, the powerless and the chancers gravitated together, formed loose gangs and gave themselves mock-heroic names – Inter City Firm (ICF), Service Crew, Headhunters... In keeping with the

Thatcherite times, the sharper characters involved in these groups managed to turn their tales of thuggery into a partial career, churning out books that spun minor incidents into wild, life-threatening melees. Some enterprising East Enders – you could tell the direction they were heading when they began producing business cards to leave with their victims – set up their own 'hooligan-style' ICF clothing line. It was more Ealing Comedy than slasher flick.

The impression of mass, organised disorder suited the police, too. New anti-hooligan units were set up and given handsome budgets. The organised crime industry had a new adjunct.

Travelling fans had two options in dealing with what was happening around them: laugh at the entire hooligan scene or become part of it. So, on every ordinary train there were those who aspired to be 'generals', who talked of 'ambushes' and 'battles'. And then there were the rest of us, who chuckled at them.

This should not be seen as denial that hooliganism existed. It did, but it was much less complex than the amateur sociologists suggested. Committed travelling fans were – and still are – generally young working-class men who, in confrontational situations, will respond with violence, the only tool many can call upon. And there was a lot of confrontation around in 1985, especially in Liverpool.

This was a place completely at odds with the political mood of the times. The city council was in conflict with Whitehall and the Militant Tendency drew strong support among young men. Like football, politics offered excitement, a bit of travel and the prospect of a rather enticing sense of lawlessness. Many who followed Liverpool – and Everton – had been involved on picket lines at Eddy Shah's plant at Warrington and later lent their support to the pitworkers during the Miners' Strike. Some were not shy about taking on the police.

The outpouring of anger was easily misread as an expression of nihilism. This is far from the truth. Punk rock had changed the landscape of youth culture and proved that creative expression was not merely the province of the effete and arty. In Liverpool, Peter Hooton, who would find fame in the late 1980s and early 1990s as lead singer and driving force of The Farm, was at the centre of a group who produced *The End*, one of the great landmarks of fanzine development.

The End, which began in 1981 – five years before *When Saturday Comes* hit the streets – was not strictly aimed at football fans but pitched at the sort of people who drank in the Yankee and the Wine Lodge, went to the match and were into music and fashion. As much as it celebrated the terrace culture, it mocked it.

The End carried a wide-ranging and funny series of pieces on bands, betting on horses, signing on the dole, drinking to oblivion and the excesses of those obsessed with designer labels. Its take on hooliganism was clear-eyed and unsentimental. Its stock characters – with names like Billy Bullshitter and Joe Wag – were caricatures of the people who lived in the same world as us. It was inspiring, celebratory and contemptuous at the same time and a brilliant reflection of a type of working-class culture that existed then, produced by people who lived the lifestyle. *The End* was angry and incomprehensible to some but its intelligence and wit shone through.

Hooton was an inspiring character and soon formed The Farm. Around him were people like Kevin Sampson, who wrote *Awaydays*, a novel about football fans that is significantly better and much more truthful than all the first-person 'I-was-top-boy' books. These were people with energy and cleverness who moved between football, music and writing with ease and captured the spirit of the time while the mainstream press was feeding the egos of the deranged and scaring its readers silly with tales of football violence. In reality, *The End* was much more threatening to middle England, tracking a deeper disaffection and anger that could not be assuaged by a brawl at a football match.

In the scoreboard end at Old Trafford in 1982, I had a chance meeting with Hooton. I was with George Maher, a mate who played the trumpet, and Hooton asked him to go along and rehearse with the band. George mentioned I was a trumpeter, too – I'd been working on

Tune A Day book one for the previous six weeks on a borrowed instrument. I was invited along and we began playing with the band.

Unlike most groups, it was hard to be sure of the dividing line between those on stage and in the audience. The boys who came to watch The Farm had the same interests as the band members: football, drink, girls and politics. After one raucous performance, one of the boys handed over the ultimate compliment: 'That was brilliant. Just like the match.' There was more to terrace culture than beatings and battles.

It was a time of great energy and excitement and a world unrecognisable from most of the shallow memoirs of scarcely reformed thugs that now define many people's image of the time. Even on the periphery of this creative uprising, it was clear to see that something new was happening. Ten years later, after Gascoigne's tears in Italy, the greater population would become comfortable with football's appeal and a generation of fanzines would cosily deal with cross-cultural themes, linking in fashion and music. Later, what was called 'laddism' became fashionable, a wealthy, watered-down version of the realities of early 1980s scally behaviour. To those of us who had read *The End* and lived in the environment it grew out of, it all looked a bit jaded, smug and middle-class.

* * *

At midnight on Friday, still more than two days from Istanbul, I was feeling a little jaded myself. Even a sleeper carriage can be trying when a train's rocking motion is stirring up the beer and sekt. Thankfully, there was a long stop. Munich. A place that holds a high position in Liverpool's European Cup mythology. There, after a 0-0 draw at Anfield in the semi-final of 1981, an arrogant Bayern were vanquished in the Olympic Stadium in a tale that had everything.

Underdogs in a hostile arena lose their main weapon and talisman in the first eight minutes. This genius is replaced by a local boy, from the wrong side of the tracks, who plays the game of his life and leaves a little bit of black-and-blue Liverpool 8 attitude tattooed on a number of

German bodies. That Howard Gayle is black – his skin colour was rare in the game back then – made it a bigger story for some. But for us it was another Scouser writing his name in our history. The 1-1 draw sent us to Paris. But, sadly for Howie, he's the second name that comes to mind when Munich is mentioned in our circles.

It's less the high drama than the low comedy that lingers in the memory. The night before the game, a number of Reds fans got into a little cultural misunderstanding that led to the usual over-reaction from the local *polizei*. The boys were rounded up, handcuffed and placed in a paddywagon. Seething at the injustice of it all, one of the crew got a little uppity and it took three or four police to manhandle him into the vehicle. Like Howie Gayle, Scrat saw his chance to take a place in history. And he seized it.

Scrat went everywhere Liverpool played. He inhabited the scally world where people existed to have a good time and go the match. He would have been at home in the pages of *The End*.

Seeing his captors distracted and at the back of the queue for the short ride to the lock-up, he took off. The handcuffs? They stayed on.

He made it back to the hotel and on to a shocked BBC news report that night. Groups of Scousers were then sent foraging across the capital of Bavaria looking for hardware shops. Without a word of German, they had long and animated conversations with sales assistants in an attempt to load up with hacksaw blades. Estimates of how long it took to cut the handcuffs off vary wildly – from six hours to two days.

Such was the reality of what the nation saw as hooliganism. The 'generals' and the sensationalist press bracketed their experiences with Henry V calling his troops to arms; the reality was of Falstaffian excess, low comedy of the basest and most pathetic sort. Hangovers and iron filings sum up the period, really. It was *Carry on Supporting* for most fans and it was a joy. But Rome changed all that for us.

It was not something to dwell on as the train headed towards the Alps, so I turned my thoughts to Dave to assure myself that there is still room for hilarity in the game today.

PART TWO

5

Nothing to see but the sand

EVEN AT 3-0 DOWN, Jamie Carragher had an aura. With hanging heads around him, he chased, howled advice and encouragement and dived into tackles with obscene commitment. When there was actually hope of winning, he found a deeper ferocity, a force of will that was fearsome. After one last-gasp challenge in the area, he rose clutching his thigh and limping. He hobbled back to position and, seconds later, was stretching the aching limb a tendon or two farther than seemed possible to make another vital interception. He knew the history; it had overshadowed every moment of his career at Anfield, where the accomplishments of the past have overwhelmed some players who have failed to emulate those achievements. Carragher wanted to match the feats of his predecessors and be remembered gloriously, not as someone who didn't quite come up to scratch. When the greats gathered, he wanted to be there, to join the most exalted of his elders on equal terms. Nothing was going to stop him. Awed by his commitment, his obvious and unsettling craving, I wondered how Dave was.

Dave had heard enough of the past, too. It haunted and mocked him. In his 30s, Dave was a rare thing in a Liverpool man: a European Cup final virgin. In his circle of acquaintances, this is tantamount to being a homosexual. Or worse. An Evertonian.

Now this made me nervous on the approach to Vienna when I pondered the subsequent journey. There are some people who can handle being a football fan and there are some who become warped and weird because of it. A psychiatrist would prescribe Dave a long period away from the game. In a padded cell.

This was a very hungry boy who never expected a feast of Turkish Delight in Istanbul. He could not really afford the trip, but sacrifices have to be made. Like the wife and children. So a cheap flight to Vienna was purchased and the plan was to busk it across the Balkans.

But the scheme had one problem. Dave had what he had wanted for two decades: a ticket for the big game. But he also had to spend two days in a sleeping compartment with a man who didn't and would, in desperate circumstances, take desperate measures to acquire one. Me.

It was hot in Vienna. At 7.30 in the morning it was more than 70 degrees. Sweating, I headed off looking to see some sights. Being keen not to appear like a tourist – especially on deserted morning streets – it was bad form to consult a map. Walk long enough, went the theory, and the Danube will be there. Of course, I'd headed in the wrong direction. There were no sights to be seen in my short excursion to the great Habsburg imperial capital. The only places open were Turkish restaurants serving migrant workers. I knew the Turks had reached the gates of Vienna in 1683 but heard they'd been locked out. Turns out that quite a few of them had bunked in.

After a fruitless hour it was easier to give up and go and wait for Dave. I expected him before midday and at 2.15 we needed to be on a train for Budapest. There was nothing to do except blend into the background with the train-station lowlife, have a drink and consider the Dave conundrum.

Even at home, there can be a wild-eyed feel about Dave that made me nervous knowing that, on past performance, it was eminently possible that we would have a misunderstanding with a Balkan policeman. Because I've seen the film. Yes, the film.

Unable to afford a trip to Cardiff for the League Cup final against Manchester United in 2003, Dave and my youngest brother decided to set up a video camera and record their responses throughout the game while they watched on television. Even before kick-off, they'd forgotten the lens was on them. What they filmed would scare even those Balkan policemen with ethnic cleansing on their resume.

Cleverly edited, the video would win an Academy Award for best short film. It shows how the veneer of civilisation is easily rubbed away. Their descent into incoherence is followed by an expression of malevolence that is as irrational as it is uncontrollable. Well, not quite irrational... it was Manchester United, after all.

Quickly, any semblance of humanity leaves these two raving monsters. The goal brings forth not joy, but the basest, rawest and most dangerous emotions. The howls are deep, visceral and spine-tingling and the human contact engendered by the goal is like a brutal form of sumo wrestling.

Suddenly, they see the camera again. Self-realisation dawns, and they turn it off, no more light to be shone on the heart of darkness.

The obvious conclusion to draw from this is that this pair are the worst sort of football hooligans. Yet nothing could be farther from the truth.

Their rage on video came from not being at the match. Every heartfelt emotion when you're watching on television is warped by the knowledge that you are not at the game, not singing about a 'Poor Scouser Tommy', but stuck in a small room at home. Possibly with a mother or wife in the same house telling you to calm down and stop swearing.

Even in defeat, it's better to have taken the journey to the match rather than staying at home. Away travel always involves a series of adventures that can be recounted for decades afterwards. What stories has Dave got to tell? Well, he's turned off plenty of televisions and gone to bed depressed.

So defeats warp Dave. Each season, as the chance of European glory disappeared, he became increasingly bitter. Even a trip to the Uefa Cup final in Dortmund in 2001 could not make up for what had been missed. The match, a 5-4 victory over Alaves, was adjudged a classic by some as Liverpool, after going 2-0 up, let the Spanish side back into the game before winning in extra time. It was an amazing spectacle but, Dave was told repeatedly, 'it's not the real thing, not like a proper European Cup final'.

Everyone was quick to remind him that one of the greatest football nights of his life was really a second-rate bit of frippery, quite unlike what we'd all seen.

So this was a boy needing release, redemption. And I was the man to show him the Promised Land. Or, maybe, nick his ticket.

Now I probably wouldn't, but Dave has been wounded before. His Dad, Big Dave, often talks about the European Cup finals. 'What a day it was in Paris,' he'll say to his son. 'I'll bet you'll never forget it.'

'I wasn't there. You never took me.'

'Who was the young lad I had with me, then?'

Who indeed? Even my mother mocks Dave. His own, too.

So, until I could come by a ticket of my own, my plan was to disturb Dave. Use the two-day journey across Eastern Europe to destabilise him by telling him stories of the great European adventures of the 1970s and 80s. He'd heard them all before, but he could never repeat them, because they weren't his tales. As the game in Istanbul gets nearer, he'll become more tightly wound and, with a little luck and some clever and timely prodding, he'll snap just in front of a Turkish black mariah.

There'll be a nice period of rest at the *Midnight Express* relaxation spa and I will find a good home for his ticket.

See how the desire to be at the match warps you?

6

Never walk alone

THERE WAS AN empty seat next to me. Where was that ticket? Who hadn't been bothered to get here? What type of tragedy had stopped them getting here? On the other hand, it wasn't exactly hardcore Scouse where I was standing, so you had to wonder whether someone just decided to watch on telly.

It was amazing to see exactly who was motivated to make the journey to Istanbul. When Gerrard pulled one back, a young man in a PSV Eindhoven shirt turned to me. His Dutch accent was almost as much of a shock as the goal. 'Ve vin now,' he stated, with a zealot's nod of the head. We?

And there he was, walking into Westbannhof station with that particular swagger football fans assume when entering railway hubs – a sort of feral crouch of the head and shoulders, eyes darting about looking for danger but with just enough of a strut to display a deterrent toughness. He looked as if he'd never passed the boundaries of Huyton before.

Now, of course Dave had been abroad. To Spain, Greece, probably, and to the States. But those were holidays and any sophistication picked up overseas didn't count in football terms. Going abroad to matches is a different experience, with different demands and rewards. Normal holidays are about relaxation and the faint dream of adventure. On a match trip, it's gruelling and adventure is almost guaranteed.

That's largely because of the way people react to you when they find out you're a football fan. They expect you to misbehave and give greater significance to minor misdemeanours that would be shrugged off if committed by any other type of tourist. Accidentally knock a glass off a bar and no one rushes to sweep away the pieces. They call the police. Suddenly it's tear gas and 26 arrests.

So Dave, at the start of the big adventure, was tense. He walked straight to where I was drinking – beside what appeared to be a betting kiosk – and said: 'Where are we going to watch the Cup Final?'

The boy was a natural. All business.

Budapest was the answer. But first we needed to eat and get as much Viennese atmosphere as possible in the 100 minutes before our train departed. Inside the first rustic restaurant we saw, it was time to turn to the local delicacies section of the menu. A special brawn for starters was followed by veal brain faggots. Dave, that unseasoned traveller, plumped for steak and chips. So began the long battle between my bowels and local colour. Funnily enough, Dave didn't have any trouble that way.

The three-hour journey to Budapest was just long enough to complain about the team's performance in the final game of the season – a 2-1 victory over Aston Villa. There are those who might suggest that signing off with a win before heading to the Champions League final gives scant grounds for complaint. They would be wrong. Moaning is a vital part of the football experience and should be developed at length. It is OK to be bullish when talking to opposing fans, but care must be taken not to show too much optimism among your own. Even if the team are the best in the world, there will always be a weak link, a whipping boy, to provide the moaners with an outlet. When the team are underperforming, any sober show of sanguinity leaves you vulnerable and likely to be punished. It was a lesson reiterated for me earlier in the season.

After a mildly encouraging away performance, I foolishly suggested to another Liverpool supporter that there were signs of improvement.

There was a contemptuous snort down the phone and a rebuke. 'I'm a very hard to please Liverpool supporter,' I was told.

As it happened, I had the ammunition to hit back. 'In 78-79, I saw all 16 league goals we conceded. Four shouldn't have gone in. That's how hard to please I am,' I said. But the damage had been done. I'd had to get the big guns out.

There's a simple logic to moaning. It's impossible to impress anyone with your football knowledge if the majority of your opinions consist of unqualified praise and eagerness. The trick is to notice a weakness in a player or team and, if you articulate it with enough conviction, most people will think you have superior insight – even if it's all invention.

For those who like living life on the edge, there's always extreme moaning, which carries the greatest risks but the greatest rewards. If, for example, you say, 'the one thing I've noticed about Michael Owen is that he's not a natural goalscorer', the listeners will either tar and feather you or, in Glenn Hoddle's case, let you continue to be England manager for a while and then employ you in the game until your energy returns to become one with the oneness at the heart of the universe.

So we ranted our way across the continent. So much so that we failed to notice we were in Hungary until our first Eastern European police-men arrived to scrutinise our passports, bark out a question in Magyar and be nonplussed by Dave's answer. 'Liverpool, going to Istanbul,' he said, with just enough of a don't-try-to-stop-me-la edge to irk a man in uniform.

As a guide to life, the best football tactics can be translated into the perfect philosophy. Pass the ball the way you're facing, move into space, keep it simple. Never try to beat one man too many. Apply those pre-cepts to any problem and the solution is obvious. Choose the most direct path, the one where you've got the clearest view, and play the easy ball. The people with complications in life are the ball-jugglers and back-heelers. Now Dave, in his excitement, has always dwelt on the ball a little, with a hefty first touch that can give himself a hospital pass. He retained possession this time – the border guard had a disposition that suited a sunny afternoon – but it does make those alongside him nervous.

The train pulled into Budapest and the passengers moved along the carriage to the doors. We did likewise. The station looked like a Cold War cliché – battered, deserted and as far from a main line terminal as possible. A nice gentleman held the door for me as I humped my bag down, saying in English: 'Let me help.'

'I'm aright, mate,' I said, struggling with a knee that had locked up at the sight of steps. Dave followed me, again with the smiling man holding the door. While I was looking for the way out, Dave voiced my concerns. 'Is this the right place?'

Our friend now nipped back up the stairs and said: 'This is not the main station.' He shut the door and the train pulled out. 'You need the next stop,' he shouted. 'You are at the wrong place.'

Annoying, but the minor delay would not bother us. And our mischievous helper was wrong. I've been in wrong places before and this was not one of them. And, as if reading my mind, Dave asked: 'What was Turin like?'

7

To the gates of Rome

MENTAL STRENGTH IS invariably more important than raw talent in top-level sports and that was showing. Milan, who had eased their way around the pitch and picked holes in the defence at will, suddenly looked disorganised, confused and frightened. When the ball dropped to Vladimir Smicer – a player not lauded for psychological robustness in his six years at Anfield – there looked to be little danger. Yet he shot anyway. Just as we began to groan that the attack had petered out, Dida, the Brazilian goalkeeper, got his dive completely wrong and almost helped the ball into the net. The celebrations in the stand were truncated by a surge of belief that buzzed among us. 'Come on,' a man behind me called. 'They're shithouses. They're Italian. They always run away.' It was poor taste. The knockout stages of the competition had been dominated by our relationship with Italians. And, from bitter experience, some of us knew the comment wasn't true.

It had to happen one day, but no one was prepared for it on March 18, 2005. At the quarter-final draw, Liverpool came out first and then Juventus. Twenty years on from Heysel and the 39 deaths at that European Cup final, the two sides were facing each other for the first time. How the teams could have failed to engineer a match before, to find some level of rapprochement, seems ludicrous but no one wanted to think about what happened in Brussels two decades earlier – not Uefa, the clubs or their fans. The only people who kept what happened to the forefront of their minds were the families of the dead, who had been fighting for recognition and justice to no avail.

In 1985, there were a few attempts by the people of Liverpool to reach out to Turin. Peter Hooton was instrumental in bringing over a group of young Italians to the city, where they were treated to a cruise on the Mersey, with John Peel as disc jockey and The Farm performing live. The crowd was emotional and keen to put the youngsters from Piedmont at ease. However, it was a night of outstanding drunkenness and featured the sort of shenanigans that sent Peel back to London shaking his head in amazement. There was no violence, but the inebriated abandon probably confirmed every prejudice the Turin teenagers had against Scousers. Others tried to build bridges, too, but without the clubs involved, it was an uphill task.

Otello Lorentini, whose son Roberto died at Heysel, had long campaigned for the clubs to play a friendly match in tribute to those killed. Roberto was a doctor and was giving one of the injured mouth-to-mouth resuscitation when the wall collapsed and the tumble of brickwork and people came smashing down. Like the other 38, Roberto had been forgotten by the world at large.

Most of us had reached an accord with ourselves over the years. It was easy to rationalise for Liverpool supporters. The fault lay with Uefa for scheduling such a big game in a stadium that was so transparently ill-equipped to hold it. A wall collapsed. If the wall had done its job, no one would be dead and the past 20 years would have been very different. It had been said a million times on Merseyside and any debate ended with a shrug.

The twentieth anniversary was due in May, at the end of Champions League final week, so there had been some stirrings of regret and remembrance, but it was hard to think too much about Heysel before April 15, when we had our own disaster to mourn. Now the draw had left us with no choice. Heysel had emerged from a collective memory lapse but, if fate and Uefa had kept Liverpool and Juventus apart, most people would have been happy to ignore the issue for another 20 years.

It was time to face up to the past.

But before we got to Brussels, or Turin, there was Rome. In this place of so many historic events, what happened to us in the Eternal City changed the nature of Liverpool's support in Europe and had consequences that were still rumbling on in Istanbul.

* * *

Rome has never been a centre of football power. Before 1980, Lazio and AS Roma, the city's largest clubs, had won the domestic title just once each. So it was unfortunate that the European Cup final should be scheduled for Rome's Olympic Stadium in 1984, the year after Roma won the league and qualified for the competition.

Playing such a huge game at a team's home stadium should not have been allowed to happen, but Uefa has never shown the greatest ability to apply common sense. Even today, the risk of a similar situation occurring is taken almost every year. The inevitable happened in 1984 and Roma reached the final, along with Liverpool. Uefa probably thought it was entirely in keeping with the city's reputation for throwing people to the lions.

The headlines in the Roman papers said: 'The Barbarians are coming,' which was worrying. A riot when tickets went on sale at the Olympic stadium increased the sense of foreboding and barely more than 8,000 fans travelled to Italy to support Liverpool. More than 25,000 had made their way to the city seven years earlier when it was a neutral venue and headed off home flushed with victory and the praise of the local police and politicians. This was a special place for Liverpool fans, the stadium where the greatest feat in the history of the club had been achieved. All fondness for the city itself would evaporate on one terrifying night.

From the moment we landed at a small airport some way from the city it was clear that it was going to be a long and difficult day. Paramilitary police in combat fatigues and riot gear met us and loaded us onto buses. Those who were hoping to see the Sistine Chapel complained until they saw the reception we got on the ring road.

Carloads of youths in cloth-topped Fiats shadowed the coaches, pulling alongside while an occupant popped up through the roof to fire a flare or hurl a brick at the bus – all at motorway speed. Burgundy and yellow flags were everywhere in the blocks of flats that sit on the seven hills and there was a clear feeling that the result was a formality. Liverpool could not win. We were taken to a disused funfair and kept there under armed guard for most of the afternoon.

So we sat and drank beer. Bored, we decided to see if it was possible to get away and see some of the sights. The carabinieri were surprisingly amenable to us leaving. 'Wanna go the Vatican, mate,' I said, blessing myself. The policeman pointed up the street. After two steps, we were going no farther. In the direction the man had indicated stood a huge mob of Roma fans, who immediately became alert when we came into sight. We went back into the funfair. I blessed myself again, indicating that I was praising the Lord for seeing me through the valley of the shadow of death. The policeman smirked. He understood.

We arrived at the ground 90 minutes before kick-off and what we found in the streets around the stadium unsettled us even more. They were deserted. Only Scousers wandered about, but what they had to say was unpleasant. There had been much trouble in the tourist areas, with gangs of locals on scooters chasing down small groups or stragglers among the Liverpool fans and slashing them as they passed. Often, at away games, there were expansive rumours about stabbings and beatings but they almost always came from the proto-hooligans. Here, they were coming from reputable sources. We found a bar, not far from the stadium and had a final drink in the beer garden. There, we relaxed. Despite the pastoral setting, it was like the Yankee. As we walked in, '*I am a Liverpudlian* started. Hands on hearts, we joined the thrilling, discordant cacophony and the worries evaporated temporarily. Not everyone was happy though. A 'Munich' song began, mocking the 1958 air disaster that killed seven Manchester United players and a number of others after a botched takeoff in Bavaria.

> 'Up, down,
> Swooping around,
> Looping the loop
> And then hitting the ground.
> How I wish I had seen,
> Those Mancunian c**** crash their flying machine.'

A middle-aged man with a Lancashire accent came out of the bar and called all the singers 'scum' before quickly disappearing to catcalls. It just made everyone laugh. The songs were funny, we thought, and we hated United.

That vignette sums up the era. The song, repugnant and offensive as it is, was chanted in a setting where it was extremely unlikely to lead to confrontation. For those outside the small world of ordinary trains and the Yankee, it enhanced the image of violent, unpleasant hooliganism in action. The singers liked to be viewed this way – outside the law, at odds with society. It felt good to be outlaws, even if most would never throw a punch at an opposing supporter. What was more important was the shared knowledge, the sense of exclusivity, the feeling of belonging. It was naughty, but for the most part pathetically and stupidly innocent.

What innocence we had, we were about to lose. Real violence was literally around the corner.

Inside the ground it was back to reality. There were people with bruised faces and patched-up shallow slash wounds that they dismissed as deep scratches; proof, if we needed it, that there was the potential for violence here on a scale to which we were unused.

We had barely got through the turnstiles when we met John, whose father is Italian. He'd travelled by train, stayed with relatives near Turin and had driven to Rome with a couple of cousins. He explained why the streets were deserted. Italian fans, he said, like getting inside the ground early. His cousins had insisted that he go into the stadium three hours before kick-off. 'We were the only ones in our end for two hours,' John said, aggrieved. 'I didn't mind the abuse of the whole ground, but I didn't like the flares.' Every Roma nutter with a firework had set his sights on this pathetic little group.

There had been plenty of action once the main body of Liverpool fans arrived. A hail of missiles came from the Roma fans adjacent to the away section, so the police baton-charged the foreigners. Stevie, another mate, had seen his camera broken by an Italian nightstick. There was no protection. The police felt like another arm of Roma's hooligans.

A volley of flares thrilled the locals and they began to sing, a noise as fearsome as in any ground I've visited – and this without a roof to funnel the noise. Thankfully, the game took our mind off the reaction on the terraces.

The match ended in a 1-1 draw and went to penalties. Steve Nicol missed the first and the Roma fans celebrated like the cup was theirs. However, Bruno Conti and Francesco Graziani also missed and the Liverpool end went crazy.

I have a photograph taken a moment after Alan Kennedy had scored the decisive penalty to seal the victory. While friends and family celebrate to the camera, I am standing in the background, looking away with a strange expression on my face. I was watching the angry Roma supporters throw their scarves and banners into piles and set them alight before leaving. It was surreal. A ring of fire hemmed us in. I know exactly what I was thinking: Shit, we've got to leave the stadium and go outside soon.

Some 20 minutes later, as we walked up a ramp to road level, the attack started. Metal bins were set aflame and hurled down the steep grass verges, supplemented by bricks, bottles and sticks. At street level, the

Romans charged, a surge that seemed uncomfortably well timed to coincide with tear gas the police shot into the rear of the Liverpool fans. As a contribution to crowd control, it was not the *carabinieri's* finest hour.

From behind came another roar. 'We're screwed,' I remember saying to no one. And then more Italians arrived, only this time wearing the light blue scarves of Lazio. They were coming to our aid – or at least to fight the Roma. Either way, those of us who had any sense – or were in the right position – made their escape in the confusion.

At the relative safety of the coach, I needed to empty a nervous bladder. As I moved into the bushes, Big Al came with me, 'just in case'. It was just as well. A few seconds into the piss, he called out my name. Behind me, 15 yards or so away, were two Italians in Roma ski hats and one had a knife. I turned, shouted, peed all over my trousers and watched them weigh up the situation and decide to back away. As a general rule, I'd advise against getting into circumstances where you're facing a man with a knife and your knob is hanging out.

Everyone on the coach had a good chortle at me, but the laughter was panicky. People were very scared. However, bravado grew in direct correlation with our distance from the ground and by the time we reached the airport some of the shirt-wearers were claiming to have 'run the Roma'. It was typical. The big talk of football supporters rarely had a mooring in reality.

Back in Liverpool, the local news said that about 10 fans had been stabbed. Then, the night after the match, we saw Ian being interviewed. He didn't say much and had a large plaster across a broken nose. What he said when he came home was shocking.

Ian was the youngest of three brothers, the eldest, Kevin, being part of our little group of match-goers. We'd bump into Stephen, the middle brother, at away games. George, their father, was a fine man, strong, full of integrity and not to be trifled with.

Once, he happened upon some Liverpool supporters beating up a Manchester United fan. He could not walk on. He dragged the youth from the fray, ignored the insults and took him home before seeing him to Lime Street in a taxi. In Rome in 1984, he again saw something he could not let pass.

A large group of Italians were kicking a boy in a red shirt all over the street. This was at a time when the majority of Liverpool fans were backing off, trying to get away from the violence. George didn't and dragged the lad, who happened to be Italian, away from the mob. But in the moments it took, the police and away supporters had disappeared. Only predatory, angry Roma fans remained. 'We had our backs to the river,' Ian said. 'And hundreds of them just stood there, looking at us.'

There were police lines not far away, and father and son decided the only way out was to head in that direction at full pelt. 'In Britain, you would have met a wall of kicks and punches,' Ian said. 'But the mob opened up, swallowed us, and the next thing I know they were kicking me and hitting me with branches.'

His father had somehow managed to push back the crowd, pick up two branches – which the Roma fans had stripped off trees before the game to use as weapons – and rush over to attempt to rescue his son. 'The crowd split and as he was telling me to get up, a young lad ran across behind him. I could see the knife. He stabbed him hard here.' Ian gestured to the lower back, in the area of the kidneys. 'The blade went all the way in.'

Helped up by his dad, Ian rose and stumbled across to two policemen who were sitting on the bonnet of a squad car some 20 yards away. 'They'd seen it all,' Ian said. In the few short steps, it was clear that George was losing a lot of blood. Ian gestured to the policeman to help. He was shocked by the response. 'The copper punched me in the nose,' Ian said.

Farther down the road, another policeman reacted differently. He threw George into the back of a squad car and rushed to hospital. There, Ian recalled, 'there were about 80 or 90 Liverpool fans all bleeding, lying all over the floor'. One by one they disappeared over the next few hours until he was alone. He was 17 years old.

'The doctors couldn't speak English,' he said. 'There was a lot of head-shaking. A nun came in and the nurse sent her right across to me. She couldn't speak English, either, but I was sure he'd died.'

For Ian, the nightmare continued until he was taken to see his father the next day after an operation. George had barely survived and it took him a long time to get back on his feet. This was the worst story, but across Liverpool similar tales were being told and smaller scars and bruises displayed. None of us wanted to see another Italian again. But, by God, if we did, we'd be ready for them next time.

8

The team that we all know

NOW THE IMPOSSIBLE was on. Across the stadium Liverpool fans squirmed, pinched and cramped by nervous tension. At the other end, no doubt our Milan counterparts were experiencing similar pain. And everyone was praying. 'Please God,' someone standing near hissed, and those who weren't saying it aloud were offering deals up to heaven in exchange for another goal.

And football does this on a weekly basis. It makes the godless and religious alike turn to prayer. When Gerrard went into the box and went down under a challenge from Gattuso, the incantations went into overdrive. The referee had blown for a foul, but from our position it was not clear which way the decision would go. Carragher charged down the official, vividly gesticulating his annoyance. Could it be because the foul was against us?

The impossible had already happened. Atheists, agnostics and devil-worshippers alike were calling on a deity to influence a decision in a game. Lip-reading those around me, it was clear that there was more focused prayer than at a Billy Graham revival. But why would God care?

The FA Cup Final was on our mind as we finally drew into Budapest. However, it quickly became clear that there was no chance of watching the match. The train, direct to Istanbul, that we'd been booked on at home, didn't exist. The Bucharest train left in less than an hour and there was confusion over whether the sleeper ticket we carried was valid.

There was only time to buy beer, bread and sausages, amend the carriage arrangements – not quite so simple with the impenetrable clash of Scouse and Magyar – and get settled for the overnight haul to Romania.

News from Cardiff was relayed through text messages. But we were thinking of a different match. Two men, trapped in a train, and only one precious ticket. Thoughts darkened with the dusk. Someone could step off the carriage at a boondock station and miss the departure. It could take days to get back to civilization. Especially if the person involved was bound and gagged…

'What if you don't get in?' Dave asked. Had he read my thoughts?

'I'll get in.'

But there's always a hint of nervousness. The authorities fear travelling fans without tickets more than any other sort, so try to discourage people from attempting such a journey. They issue press releases that promise dire consequences for anyone not carrying tickets. A favourite is that you'll be turned back at borders – and if you do get through, you'll be arrested by the local police or refused entry by bars, hotels and restaurants. In reality, matches at neutral venues – even finals – often do not sell out. It was clear that demand for this game was unusually huge on the Liverpool side, but the Ataturk Stadium's location, plus the nervousness of Milan supporters, meant that there would be empty seats on Wednesday.

So, on Saturday night, we waited for news from Wales and cheered when Arsenal beat Manchester United on penalties. Our satisfaction did not come out of love for Arsenal.

If the train between Paris and Vienna could evoke an opulence beyond the ken of someone from Liverpool's docklands, the sleeper here was of a different standard. A carpeted bench served for a single seat and no linen was supplied for the mattress. Turkish tobacco and sweat had seeped into every fixture and fitting. It reminded me of the flophouse bed-and-breakfasts around King's Cross where we'd sleep off the drink before big games in London in the days when £8 a bed seemed extravagant.

Outside, we watched the gloom settle in across pastoral rural landscapes as peasants dressed like anachronistic ghosts rode ponies and carts on dirt roads. The terrain was lush and delectable from a distance but when the train slowed near towns or villages, it appeared that any convenient area had been turned into a makeshift midden. These people were poor, alright. And then I thought of the mile-and-a-half walk from home to Anfield, of the deteriorating streets either side of Scotland Road, of the jungly, rubbish-strewn rubble between Great Homer Street and Netherfield Road and the lines of burnt-out and boarded-up houses on the approach to the Kop and felt a little less smug. These people would recognise the worn, beaten faces from back home.

With night, we bedded down. Three days from Lime Street, 30 hours from Istanbul.

Living in the European Union, it's easy to forget about borders. Now we got a reminder. The authorities in this part of the world specialise in torture by sleep deprivation. Just after we'd dropped off, a knock came on the door. The guard was waking everyone ready for our imminent arrival in Romania and collecting passports. First though, came the Hungarians. The police arrived, took a look at us, asked our nationality and moved on. Some 10 minutes later passport control turned up, stamped our documents and asked us where we were going and left, still scrutinising the photos. Dave was dazed, but I noticed he was sleeping in his trousers. What was he expecting? A gay pass?

More than half an hour after the conductor's knock, customs arrived. They asked the same questions as their four colleagues, took a perfunctory look at our bags and left. Finally, we moved on. About 100 yards. And there the same process began again, with the Romanians performing the same duties as if learnt from the same script. Now I could see why these journeys took all night.

Perhaps it was a hangover from the Cold War. Get the sleep deprivation in early – makes the interrogation easier later on. The whole process took the best part of two hours. It was raining heavily even though the temperature was unpleasantly high. Opening the window brought water into the carriage; leaving it closed helped add another splash of sweat to further marinade the mattress. The acute level of discomfort was entirely in keeping with my experiences as a travelling fan.

'Read your Heysel stuff,' Dave said. I'm sleep deprived, and he's turned my own tactic of talking about the past back on me. The events of May 29, 1985, have coloured the entire run to Istanbul. We'd like to forget it, but we don't have a prayer.

9

What should have been a joyous time

YES, IT'S A PENALTY but a new terror took over as Xabi Alonso put the ball on the spot. He took a short run, shot to the goalkeeper's right and Dida saved. Horror. For a split-second. Because Alonso came hurtling towards the rebound and, under pressure from defenders and keeper, crashed the ball in. We were level. Five hours later, in an Irish bar on an Istanbul back street, we saw the replay. When Dida saved, I had a panic attack. In my mind, there was no save; Alonso's penalty went straight in. The memory plays funny tricks. It can block out whatever it wants.

Just before 6am on May 30, 1985, on a ferry limping across the Channel, Robert, a big Ulsterman, woke me. He handed me a beer. Shivering and in the throes of the worst hangover I'd experienced to date, I shook my head.

'You'll need it,' he said. He led me to a television, where the news was about to start. 'Forty-two Italians killed in riot at Heysel,' the presenter said.

Appalled, I took a large swig of beer and then rushed to the toilet to vomit. It felt like every muscle was tearing as the dry-retching hee-hawed louder and louder.

It took a while to compose myself but when I did there was an acquaintance in the toilet, grinning at my discomfort. 'What do you think?' I asked, rinsing my face and fighting another heave.

'Shocking,' he said. 'It was never a penalty.' Off he went laughing.

* * *

The year that followed the European Cup final in Rome in 1984 was as bleak as any in Merseyside's recent history. Unemployment was chronic and common – I knew young men in their mid-20s who had not worked legally since leaving school. The Government were embroiled in a battle with the City Council that was growing more fractious. There was even talk of suspending the local authorities and bringing the army on to the streets. We all made sure we knew how to make petrol bombs.

On a national scale, the Miners' Strike had split the country and violent images from the picket lines were on television every night. Blood flowed nightly in Belfast and Derry. It felt, at least in my circles, like revolution and civil war were at hand. And we expected to be the losers.

Football, which should have been a welcome distraction, made everything worse. Liverpool supporters were bitter at the way the trouble in Rome had been reported – or not reported, from our point of view – in the national press. There was a feeling that if it had happened to any other club, people from any other city in Britain, then there would have been outrage in the papers and questions in Parliament. Like the miners, though, we were the 'enemy within'. The standing of the city was endorsed by an *Observer* review front page piece on the Northeast, which said gratuitously: 'The way the Liverpool accent is associated with violence, the Newcastle accent is…'

Football was at a low point, too. Hooliganism appeared rampant. It seemed that the only people who went to games were thugs. The mock-heroic gibbering on the trains had slipped into the general domain and the media and their consumers took it at face value. There was a growing sense of anarchy that drew more youths towards the trouble. Organised hooliganism was becoming a self-fulfilling prophecy.

In early April, it became clear that Liverpool would be playing Juventus in the European Cup final in Brussels. The words that had become a catchphrase for the year began to look ominous: 'No Italian will do that to us again.' The events in Rome were a bad memory but, fertilised by fear, they had grown into overpowering and filthy legend.

Three days after the first leg of the European Cup semi-finals, which effectively settled both ties, there was another semi-final, this time in the FA Cup against Manchester United at Goodison Park. The teams had tossed a coin to see which city should host the game. Liverpool won.

It is difficult to explain what happened at Goodison that day. There has always been an antagonistic relationship between the two cities, with the industrial centre that grew around Manchester needing and resenting the port of Liverpool. Although the rivalry has its roots in economic competition, the football teams became a focus for resentment and hostility. Even now, both Manchester clubs have a sailing ship on their badges – the ship canal was an attempt to undermine a real maritime city.

The power of the Mersey port over the Lancashire hinterland may have disappeared, but the residual hostility remains. The enmity of the football fans from the respective cities has grown to unacceptable levels down the years, especially between Liverpool and United.

Yet the events at Goodison Park in 1985 exploded into insanity on a different scale. All the anger, bitterness and fear that infused daily life suddenly dovetailed into an uncontrollable rage that hinged itself to a football match.

Supporters from both sides fought, stabbed and hurled missiles at each other throughout the day. Inside the ground, there was brawling in every section, with magnesium flares fired into crowds from close range and golf balls studded with six-inch nails flung at the opposition pens. These were not the gangs of elite, hard-core hooligans that had become a fixture in the popular imagination; these were ordinary men – and some women – caught up in madness. Liverpool were a goal down early but scored a last-gasp equaliser to take the game into extra time. United scored again and another very late goal made it 2-2. From a crowd control perspective, it was the worst way the game could have developed.

That night the Yankee was out of control. They were singing the full repertoire of Munich songs. A manic joy surged in the voices of the boys.

For once we were not joining in. I said to Big Al: 'It went too far today. Everyone lost perspective.' He agreed. Neither of us were fighters, but we moved easily in the scally world and yet we were unnerved. One of the more dangerous characters we knew passed by. 'What the fuck happened today?' he asked, awestruck. There was no answer. But this was not funny. The city was rancid with aggression.

As we left for Al to get the last bus home near 11pm, a group of dolled-up girls, carrying their high heels even at this early stage of the night, passed us singing: 'Who's that dyin' on the runway...'

Everyone expected a repeat performance for the semi-final replay at Maine Road in Manchester, but both sides seemed to realise the enormity of what had happened four days earlier and the game passed off without trouble. Liverpool lost and thoughts turned back to Brussels. On the trains, in the bars, it was said over and over: 'It won't be like Rome.'

* * *

On a sunny Brussels morning, there was a moment that, more than anything that would happen over the ensuing 24 hours, continues to haunt me. Our train had just arrived at Jette station and a long column of Liverpool supporters set off downhill towards the centre of the city. I lingered and watched them, chequered flags flying, and thought it looked like a medieval army on the move. Above the narrow street, the locals hung out of open windows and watched, half-grinning but nervous. As I set off for the Grand'Place, I thought: 'We can do what we like today. No one can stop us.'

The mood in Brussels was complex. In the aftermath, most commentators would ignore the effect of the events in Rome the previous year and even those who alluded to 1984 saw Heysel in terms of 'hooligan gangs looking for revenge'. It was very different, much more complex and consequently more frightening.

We were radiating aggression. The ultras had made us suffer once, but it would not happen again. There were few direct attacks on opposition supporters, but there was an eagerness to take the upper hand in any potential conflict. No one wanted to be a victim. Minor misunderstandings quickly escalated into full-scale confrontation, much to the shock of the Italians.

Turning into a narrow street in the centre of town, my brother and I saw about six Juventus fans in their twenties lounging outside a cafe, trying to look cool and tough at the same time. When one looked me straight in the eye, giving me a classic hard-case once-over, I snarled: 'Go on gobshite, say something.' They did not take up the offer. But the tone was set.

And the drinking had not even started.

The Grand'Place was less tense than might have been expected. Liverpool fans were here in numbers and small groups who had travelled independently met up, felt safe and relaxed into an afternoon of drinking. Clustered around the bars, we sang, bare-chested in the sun and, briefly, bonhomie abounded. It was almost idyllic. The morning had passed off quietly and the fear of ultras began to dissipate. Juventus fans ran across the square with their forty-foot Piedmont flags merging seamlessly with the seventeenth-century backdrop. It was breathtaking.

Then the drink kicked in.

The common belief was that Belgian beer was weaker than the booze at home. In the heat, young men used to drinking a gallon of weak mild were quaffing strong lagers and ales as if they were lemonade. Small incidents started to mushroom and suddenly the mood changed and the bars began to shut down. By now, there were four of us in our little group. We were reluctant to leave the square because other friends were probably heading for the rendezvous. I went to find some beer, taking a red-and-white cap I'd found on the road to give some protection from the sun. Walking down a narrow street, I saw a crew of scallies laughing almost hysterically. Seeing my quizzical look, they pointed at a shop. It was a jeweller with no protective metal grating over the window.

All you could do was laugh.

Farther on, I saw a group of Juventus supporters, and one was wearing a black-and-white sun hat. It would give me more cover in the heat, so I swapped with him.

Only he clearly did not want to part with his headwear. He had no choice. Sensing danger, he let me have it and looked in disgust at the flimsy, filthy thing I'd given him.

This was not cultural exchange: this was bullying, an assertion of dominance. I remember strutting away, slowly, the body language letting them know how I felt.

There was a supermarket by the bourse and, at the entrance, there stood a Liverpool fan. 'You're Scouse?' he said. There was no need for an answer and he knew what I was there for. 'It's free to us today,' he said, handing me a tray of beer. The rule of law was over.

On the way back to the square, the group of Liverpool fans by the jeweller had been replaced by riot police. Glass was scattered all over the street, studded with empty display trays. There was hysteria -and pride - in my laughter. This was turning into an excellent day.

We set off for the ground and there seemed to be more and more small confrontations. On other days any cultural misunderstandings would end in hugs and an exchange of memorabilia. Here, with the hair-trigger tempers, it was tears, and we were determined they would not be ours.

We boarded a tram to head north to the ground, slurring and swearing and exuding threatening, drunken boorishness. At our stop, we stood up to get off and Robert collapsed, the alcohol that had been nastily overriding a collective sense of decency was now severing the physical links between brain and body. We hauled him from the middle of the road towards the stadium, two of us with his arms over our shoulder while his feet dragged behind. He appeared unconscious. Then, on the approaches to the ground, a group of young men up ahead snatched the takings from a stallholder and ran away with his strongbox. The man went in pursuit, leaving the stall unattended. Without seeming to open his eyes, Robert deftly unhooked his arm from around my shoulder and pocketed a Juventus scarf. It was unbelievable. He immediately resumed his comatose state and we dragged him on until we reached a grass verge to lay him down.

Similar madness was everywhere. People were staggering, collapsing, throwing up. A large proportion of Liverpool fans seemed to have lost control.

We met a group of mates who had come by coach. A fellow passenger we all knew had leapt off as soon as they arrived and attacked two people, one an Italian, with an iron bar. That we'd long believed him to be psychotic did not lessen the shock.

John, who had been in the line of fire in Rome the year before, dodging flares in the empty Liverpool section, was greeting Juventus fans in heavily Scouse-accented Italian. Naturally friendly, he is a man almost incapable of violence. A group wearing Liverpool shirts attacked him and beat him to the floor. 'I'm Scouse,' he was shouting. Few people have a stronger accent.

'No you're not, you Wop,' they said. It took a riot policeman to rescue him. We thought it was hilarious.

What wasn't funny was the state of the stadium. Even in a drunk and deranged state, it appalled us. The outer wall was breeze block and some of the ticketless were kicking holes at its base and attempting to crawl through. Most were getting savage beatings from the riot police, who were finally making their presence felt. It was easier to walk into the ground and ignore the ticket collector, some of whom were seated at what looked like card tables. I went home with a complete ticket. Four years later, on another dreadful day, I would enter another ground without needing to show my ticket. It is not just the Belgians whose inefficiency had deadly consequences.

Inside the stadium, we sat the still inert Robert down and waited until he woke up. He emerged from his torpor with a start and was shocked by the Juventus scarf.

'You robbed it,' I said.

'Oh, no.' He was appalled. 'I didn't hit an Italian, did I?'

'No. It's new. You robbed it in your sleep from a stall.'

'Thank God I didn't hurt anyone,' he said. 'I think I was out of control.'

Section Y, where we were standing, grew more and more crowded and, in front of us, a crush barrier buckled and collapsed. Next door, Section Z was supposedly a neutral area. It looked to be mainly Italian, with plenty of room available. We eyed the space with envy.

The rough treatment by police drew a response and most disappeared from the back of the section after skirmishes. Seeing a policeman beating a young lad who was attempting to climb over the wall and was caught in the barbed wire, I pushed the Belgian officer away. He turned to hit me with his baton and I punched him - not hard - through his open visor. He ran away. It was the second time I'd hit someone in almost 10 years of travelling to football matches – and the other punch was aimed at a Liverpool fan.

With the police gone, groups of youths swarmed over a snack stand and looted it. I climbed on to the roof and was passed up trays of soft drinks to hand around. It felt like being on top of the world up there.

Back on the terraces there was an exchange of missiles - nothing serious by the standards of the day. I went to the toilet and, by the time I came back, the fence was down and people were climbing into the neutral section. Unable to locate my group, I joined the swarm. In section Z I wandered around for a while. There seemed to be very little trouble. People backed away but there were no charges, just a minor scuffle or two.

I climbed back into section Y, unaware that 39 people were in the process of dying. It was clear that a huge commotion was going on at the front and we began to get tetchy about the delayed kick-off.

Then there seemed to be a long tirade in Italian over the public address system - someone suggested it was a list of names - and all hell broke loose. Juventus fans came out of their end, around the pitch and attacked the corner where other Liverpool supporters were standing. My mother, youngest brother and sister were in that section.

Everyone went crazy. Men tore at the fences to get at the Italians and, at last, the police did an effective job of holding back Liverpool fans. The brother with me said: 'If those fences go, football will be finished. There'll be hundreds dead. It will be over.' Finally, the police drove the Italians back.

The game? Juventus won 1-0, with a plainly unfair penalty, and the team celebrated wildly on the pitch. There appeared to be as much joy on the terraces. That added to the shock later. Surely no one could have been badly hurt before the game if the players reacted like they did when they received the cup? How naive we were.

Afterwards? Tiredness kicked in with the disappointment but the nervousness over Italian knives lingered. A Belgian policeman gave us a send-off from the stadium by opening the bus doors, throwing in a canister of tear gas and locking everyone in.

At Ostend it was a passive, depressive struggle through overcrowded departure rooms. The police were angry, aggressive and scared. They made sure their guns were very visible and kept dogs snapping at the Liverpool fans. 'You were glad enough to see us in 1944, you fuckers,' someone said. No one mentioned death.

When the news spread on the boat there was silence and head-shaking. The enormity was overwhelming. How did this happen? The unspoken question perplexed everyone.

But instead of admitting our own culpability, seeing how our bad attitudes and fear created a situation where people would die, we immediately found other guilty parties to blame and put the victims out of our minds. Hillsborough brought some empathy for those who died at Heysel. But even that was paltry to the point of insult. Now the dead reached across two decades to knock people out of complacency.

PART 3

10

And we've been to Europe, too

RELATIVITY HAD BEEN suspended. Three goals, but how long to go? The scoreboard and the watch suggested that Liverpool had drawn level in just six minutes. It couldn't be right. Surely it was more like 25? A text came through: 'The best six minutes of my life.' Then the reverse side of the equation took effect. As the team took stock and realised the improbability of what they'd achieved, a fear began to creep in that it could be lost so easily. So, instead of pressing home their advantage, they slowed the pace. Time began to drag. The next half-hour crawled, clearly taking in the missing 20 from earlier on.

'Thank God we weren't in Bert Trautmann class,' Dave, rubbing his neck on a grim and rainy Bucharest platform, said. Lack of sleep had made us tetchy and this was not a welcoming environment at 7.30 on a Sunday morning. The only place open was McDonald's. The journey was beginning to feel onerous.

After confirming a place on the 2.30 express to Istanbul, we considered our options. A wash would be nice and a stroll around the city. We had to live without the wash.

Outside the station we were approached by a taxi tout, who clearly believed that we were Americans. 'Yankee, I give you tour,' he said.

'What do you reckon?'

'He seems to know the Yankee. Well, never been kidnapped before. Let's give it a try.'

So into the back of a taxi we climbed, with a sullen and brutish driver and our ratlike little tout acting as tour guide. 'You give me ?100,' he said.

'You show us a good time,' I countered. 'That could be taken the wrong way,' I warned Dave.

But he did.

It was a slow start, though.

Nicolae Ceausescu set the agenda. The first stop was the dictator's masterpiece, Casa Poporului, the People's House, a building only the Pentagon can outdo for size. The men had a curious mixture of pride and disgust for Ceausescu. 'He rebuild city,' the tout said. We went to two of Ceausescu's palaces, the graveyard where he is buried – or was it his family, we weren't sure – then the boulevard where the revolution started.

'Was it better when he was in power?' Dave asked.

'I had job,' the tout replied, flatly, so we were none the wiser.

The men argued for a while, forgetting the tour, as we passed down wide boulevards and crossed huge squares that made us feel like we were in Paris. We passed a cemetery, where coffin makers had set up beside the road and were pitching for business, waving down passers-by and sizing them up with a tape measure. It was interesting and quite a laugh, but this pair were coming up well short of ?100.

We arrived outside a graveyard for Italian soldiers who died in the Second World War. 'Your point, sir?' Dave asked, very formally.

'Nah, mate, not interested, we were on the other side,' I chimed in.

And as if in response to this, the tout said: 'You understand, Ceausescu very bad. But things not like now. Good to kill Ceausescu but things change for bad…'

We had thought it was funny to act like Americans and wave big notes in front of men like this, but now we felt uncomfortable.

'Yankees no understand.'

Too true. The complex relationship between people and their Governments, whether radical or based on patronage, communist or capitalist, takes more than a taxi ride to assess. Even in the half-hour we'd been with these men, their sense of loss was compelling. Yet they were reluctant to wish for the old days. And when the morning looked like stalling, Dave had a stroke of genius. He passed the ball the way he was facing.

'Gheorghe Hagi,' he said. There was a moment of silence, uncomprehending. Or maybe they thought that their former dictator was the most famous Romanian on the planet. They were wrong.

'Hagi!' he shouted. It got their attention. They repeated the great man's name, pronouncing it in the correct manner, nodding at each other and smiling.

Victoriei Square had become a sideshow. At last we were talking the same language. Next stop was Steaua Bucharest's stadium. The tout said: 'Armed guards. For ?30 I bribe.'

But we'd already gone, up the stairs, into the stands and, with no one around, dashed for the pitch. Our tout followed us. 'Champions of Europe,' he said.

'Only 'cos we were banned,' we both shot back. Steaua won the tournament in 1986, the year after Heysel. 'We're Liverpool. Going to Istanbul.'

He did not seem to understand, so he shrugged and left us Yankees to our own amusement. Actually, the stadium was a little like an American High School arena at first sight, with its new, multicoloured seats. However, the crumbling stairways spoke of neglect. The nets were still up and we both cursed our stupidity. We didn't have a ball.

It's always a serious error not to bring a ball. It is one of the fundamental items a traveller must carry. You never know on your journey through life when you'll get the chance to have a kickabout in a world-famous stadium.

However, it was enough to be there. We were giddy with excitement. When we got back to the station, we did indeed pay like Americans. The tout tried to intimidate more cash out of us but backed off when we showed no fear. The morning had turned out wonderfully after all.

Yet there was one thing that bothered us. The stadium looked very different from the place where Ian Rush scored two in the European Cup semi-final in 1984, even allowing for the filter of television. And then we realised that we'd been to the wrong stadium. It was Dinamo 21 years before, not Steaua. There was only one thing for it. Another cab.

And this time we made sure we had a ball.

Dinamo's stadium appeared from the outside to be even more ramshackle than Steaua's but with better statues. They are entirely in keeping with a Scouse view of art - muscular Soviet realism. Bill Shankly would have looked upon them with satisfaction.

It got better inside. It was set in parkland and below ground level. The bowl was sunk into the grass and trees. It was hard to see how they could limit entrance to people with tickets. What appeared to be two players were doing fitness tests on a wide v-shaped bank of stairs behind the goal that narrowed down to the pitch. The tunnel looked like a shed and who could imagine what the dressing-rooms were like? But it was hard to care when you could go down to the end where Rushie scored and slot the ball into the empty net. It was a glorious feeling. Imagine walking up to Anfield or Goodison and sloping on to the pitch for a quick game of cross and head. It was even raining, just as it was in 1984.

Overlooking Dinamo's ground are a host of tower blocks, like every young man's fantasy apartments. Open the window and you have the best seat in the house, free. Some of the blocks even have balconies and there is no roof on the stadium to interrupt the view. At Stamford Bridge they'd call these high-rises a pretentious Italian name, make you have a really crap meal and charge you six grand to watch the match.

In the club shop they had a blood-red retro Dinamo shirt in extra large. It was impossible to resist, with its pair of hunting wolves on the badge and the team name on the back. It cost less than the two cheese-burgers we'd had for breakfast and was considerably more tasteful.

By the time we returned to the station, it was abuzz with people. We discussed whether we had time to get to another stadium in the city, the home to Rapid, but decided the risk of missing the train was significant if we attempted the visit. And then Dave said, in a distracted voice: 'This is the arse end of the world.'

Eh?

'No, I mean it in the nicest possible way. Just look at the girls.'

And he was right. Even as humble a star as Kylie Minogue would throw a hissy-fit here, as her rear-of-the-year would come somewhere near the bottom of a best-in-Bucharest table. Yet there was something disturbing about the women. The well groomed and extremely pretty girls were very young; the older women were universally pug-ugly. There was no in-between and little sign of attractive women in their 30s. Either middle age has an horrible effect on Romanians, or all the pretty ones leave and take their chances in the wealthier cities of the West. You don't notice the men so much but the reasons for this are obvious.

The bright, the beautiful and the motivated up sticks in a place like this. A city that turns people into taxi touts drives away the most capable and vital of its inhabitants. I'd seen this happen. I'd been here before, some 1,500 miles to the west, on a bay off the Irish Sea. Clearly, we hadn't come so far.

11

The battle it started
next morning

EAR. PANIC. RELIEF. It all happens that quick. The mood had changed in extra time. It's a case of hanging on. Jerzy Dudek makes one save from Andriy Shevchenko but the ball falls to the Milan striker perfectly, inside the six-yard box. On an 80-degree angle from Shevchenko, it's impossible to imagine he will not score. There's only time to stop breathing as he makes contact. But the collective gasp, rather than the sight of the ball looping over the bar, explains that the score is still level. How did it happen? A Dudek save? Off the line by someone? Fear. Panic. Relief. It goes too fast for the brain to compute. How the hell did we get away with it?

Turin was just about the last place we wanted to see in 2005. Juventus, the Italian champions, were one of the favourites to win the competition and more than capable of knocking Liverpool out. Yet that was the least of it. Our shared history did not warrant a happy reunion.

Everyone accepted that a surge by Liverpool fans at the Heysel Stadium led to 39 mainly Italian supporters being crushed to death. There is a great difference in perception as to where the blame lies.

On Merseyside, the guilt was easily attributed. The disaster hinged on the collapsing wall. Had it held, no one would have died that night. Uefa and the Belgian authorities carried the blame.

In Turin, it is believed that the tumbling wall was a lifesaver. The victims were trampled or beaten to death by drunk, rampaging Liverpool thugs while they were hemmed in by fences and concrete. The weak brickwork prevented further killing.

There were darker thoughts articulated in private. Many Liverpool supporters believed that if the Italians had stood their ground in the face of the charge – half-hearted by the standards of 1985 – their compatriots would never have been crushed. In this interpretation of history, all the Second World War clichés come into play. The bullied were blamed for their efforts to avoid conflict. 'They ran away,' was said, often. 'And trampled their own.'

The sad irony is that after Hillsborough, in the quest to avoid accepting responsibility for an outrageous dereliction of duty, the police and Government put forward a version of events that pointed the finger of blame at supporters. The fury this slur caused among Liverpool fans has never abated and even though an inquiry nailed the lies, the public perception still has it that those crushed in the Leppings Lane terrace were drunk, out of control and had burst through the gates without tickets. Outside Merseyside, many people still believe that the 96 dead of Hillsborough represent some sort of payback for Heysel. The truth is that those killed in the two stadiums have never been given justice.

And some of those who felt the most anger when the guilty blamed the blameless of 1989 were still prone to sneer at the victims of 1985 and not look at their own role in an appalling sequence of events.

Immediately after the draw was made, the chatrooms on Juventus websites became filled with threats, warnings for Liverpool supporters thinking of venturing into the Stadio Delle Alpi. At least 39 of us would die, the cyberchatter said.

In Liverpool, the reactions were mixed. At the Merseyside derby, Everton fans chanted, 'Thirty-nine Italians can't be wrong' and

'Murderers'. Their team would have played in the European Cup in 1985-86 if not for the Heysel ban. They have been bitter ever since. In a leap of faith that is unfathomable to rational people, Evertonians insist that, without Heysel, their side would have won the Champions Cup in 1986 and their subsequent history would have been very different and filled with success. As a case study in how football makes people irrational, the Everton experience is illuminating. Their fans regard themselves as the true victims of the tragedy. The festering bitterness has soured relations between the city's two sets of supporters and, while the rivalry has never been quite as friendly as portrayed in the media, an unhealthy acrimony has developed in a place where families are divided by football allegiances.

For older Liverpool supporters, there was plenty of soul-searching after the draw. Finally, grudgingly, they admitted their driving role in the events that led to the deaths at Heysel. Yes, the policing was poor and the stadium woefully derelict but, without our bad attitude, the day would have passed with only a football match to recall. The *Liverpool Echo* printed a belated apology, blaring 'Sorry' from a front-page headline and the crowd at the first leg at Anfield were to hold up coloured cards to create a huge mosaic of contrition and sorrow so that the world would see we had finally repented.

Then the Juventus Ultras arrived in Liverpool.

In a city reluctant to be drawn into any kind of confrontation with them, the Juve fans behaved with truculent aggression, some of them singing songs about Hillsborough at the Albert Dock in the afternoon. It was not quite enough to provoke a police response but it showed what the visiting supporters thought of Liverpool. Scarves woven with the names of both clubs were offered to the Juventus fans and vehemently rejected. An Italian journalist who had idly draped one of these souvenirs around his neck was jostled and berated by his compatriots. These people did not want the overdue offer of friendship.

When the silence honouring the dead took place with the mass display of remorse before the game, many Juventus fans turned their backs and aimed a single middle finger in the direction of the home crowd. It looked like a warning and a statement of intent.

The timing of the second leg was portentous. It was to be played two days before the sixteenth anniversary of Hillsborough. The last thing we wanted was more bodies to bury.

On a rainy Tuesday, I walked the streets of Turin alone. There were just a handful of Liverpool supporters about – a group sang about Rafa Benitez in a bar – but few were so brazen or stupid. Small crews of locals with jackets open to show *drughi* T-shirts – one group of Juventus Ultras model themselves on Clockwork Orange imagery – appeared to be mobbing up 200 yards away. However, by the time they had the numbers to be sure of themselves, the Scousers were long gone. The habit of bar-crawling is ingrained in Liverpool men and here it worked in their favour. It was a very tense night.

Lost and unable to locate the people I'd planned to meet, I turned into a piazza about 1am. There, 50 yards or so away, were about 20 ultras, scarves pulled across their lower faces, bouncing along in that curious way young men looking for trouble cover the ground, half skipping, half shadow boxing.

They were looking for small groups of visiting supporters so there was no immediate need for panic. Relaxed body language and an unconcerned air would let me pass through them as if invisible. I'd brazened out countless situations like this over the years. They'd probably think I was an American tourist. The trick was to slow down very slightly, amble casually across the square and show a dumb confidence that this was just another bit of local colour.

Sounds easy. Except I was shitting myself.

They were gesticulating and pointing. A bigger crew came from the other side of the square. Some had sticks. They were excited, shouting to each other and pointing towards the area that contained the majority of bars. I was now in their midst.

Fighting the suicidal urge to flee, repeating the mantra, 'be calm, walk calm' in my mind, I turned into a street with the certainty of someone who knows the terrain. It was a very short dead end. It was the sort of mistake that draws attention.

As I retraced my steps back into the square, my mobile phone rang. Quite a few ultras now looked across. Clearly, I was not Italian. The only option was to answer.

'Alright, la,' I said evenly, with no attempt to keep down the volume, judging that a burst of Scouse could even be mistaken for a language other than English. It was my brother, calling from the United States. It wasn't much of a conversation, but its casual nature and a slightly forced chuckle were enough to end their interest. They were expecting the people they were looking for to behave in a different manner.

But back at the hotel it took me half an hour to stop shaking. I dreaded the next day. I'd been transported back two decades. Why the hell had I come?

* * *

Good question. Before the match, I called a mate who is far more committed to following Liverpool abroad than I am. 'No. No chance,' he said when I asked him if he was going. 'Not worth it. People will die.'

On the morning of the game the sun was out. It was the worst scenario possible. More than 3,000 away supporters were expected to arrive and if they drank and sang in the squares, gangs like the one the previous night would be sure to attack.

The paper had sent out a news reporter and photographer to cover the anticipated bloodshed and I'd got them tickets for the game. We arranged to meet for the handover and they gave me directions to a café. It was opposite the Juventus club shop, where hundreds of supporters milled about and queued for entry. Not a comfortable place for a sun-reddened Scouser. Throughout the day, I stiffened at the sound of a scooter, fighting a losing battle with body language. The news guys said they'd drive to the stadium and drop me off. At the hotel, I considered lying to them, saying I'd been called by mates and was getting on the buses provided for away fans. Then I could hole up and stay in the room until it was time to drive back to Milan airport the next day.

I met the car at the appointed time. David, the reporter, looked like an Italian. Pete had his cameras and was clearly press. I felt I had the look of a man who'd murdered 20 years ago. Pete laughed. He'd been in Sarajevo. This was just football.

There was trouble outside the ground. Two hours before kick-off, the ultras were battling with the police and the duo in the front seat headed towards where the gas canisters were flying. I was having none of it. They could go where they liked, but they were taking me to the Liverpool end or face the consequences. They could see I was serious.

We were not allowed into the Liverpool coach area, so we had to park among home fans. The police lines were a mere 50 yards away but it was a long walk. The setting sun cast long shadows and I watched for the rapid advance from behind, the one we'd lived in fear of since Rome. It never came. Safely behind the police, we parted. I went into the ground and they decided there was more chance of action outside.

The first person I saw inside was Mark. It had been a long time, perhaps pre-Hillsborough, since we last met. He now lives in Spain. 'Couldn't miss this one,' he said. 'We've all come out of retirement.'

It was a tough crew. Most, I suspect, were at Heysel. All had been irritated by the behaviour of Juventus fans at Anfield but the last thing they wanted was trouble.

'You know,' Mark said. 'You know what it's like. We'd rather not have it. If we have to have it, we'd rather have it with anyone but these. But if they want it, they're gonna get it…'

That appeared to be the general philosophy.

The mood in the stadium was not especially hostile. The banners around the ground told us that we would die - except for one that said, 'You are more ugly than Camilla', which caused general hilarity. 'We hope IRA blows you up,' another said. 'Be handling our own explosives,' someone said, laughing. Everything was quiet until about 15 minutes before kick-off.

Suddenly, the ultras threw everything they had at us. Literally. Bottles, coins, batteries and seats flew and a long-distance battle raged.

The Italians were bare-chested and frank in their fury but secure in the knowledge that no one would stop them. The police stayed at the back of the terrace and let them get on with it. The two sets of supporters could never come into contact and the stadium stewards handled the matter. They were well prepared in hard hats and only stepped in when the occasional lunatic made a solo foray too close to the fences. They seemed more worried that the madmen would scale the fence and fall to their deaths in the chasm separating the fans. These wild men were not dragged out of the ground, but merely placed back in position with their mates ready for another surge. Unbelievable. At home, behaviour like that would get you banned for life and possibly six months in jail.

It began to dawn on us that this was completely normal. Apart from the banners, they'd done nothing special for us. That would come outside, after the game, we presumed.

The cultural exchange was in full flow, but some Liverpool fans replied with more hurtful weapons than mere projectiles. Two at the front hung over the rail and made pushing motions at the Juventus supporters, as if to imply that the home fans were in retreat. At the end they flopped their hands forward to suggest a collapsing wall.

Twenty years and 96 dead of our own at Hillsborough had taught these people nothing.

The match was drab, but 0-0 sent us though to the semi-final against Chelsea. We were locked in at the final whistle, and grateful for it, despite the bravado. In the empty stadium, we sang: 'I like it, I like it, I like it, I like it - here we go, rocking all over the world.' Status Quo's song, used to celebrate Bayer Leverkusen goals and adopted by Liverpool fans after victory in Germany, kept the spirits up. Everyone suspected that in a matter of minutes we would be let out to face the hate of 20 years.

Then, after an hour, the police edged us towards the exit. Nervous tension was running high, so it was with some surprise that we found the car park deserted except for riot police. The ultras had not even stayed to harangue and harass us from a distance.

I like it, I like it, I like it!

Then I realised. That gesture eight days earlier, when the Juventus fans turned their back on Anfield's attempt at reconciliation and friendship, had been misinterpreted. In our folklore, fear of Italians has been deeply ingrained for a quarter of a century after three matches against Roma; that dread of scooters and stilettos. In facing away from Anfield's apologetic mosaic, the Juventus supporters set that fear running rampant again.

That terror built in Turin. And then nothing. The ultras did not need to fight. They had done their worst. They went to our place and showed their withering contempt for us. At the final whistle in the Delle Alpi, they threw down their flags on the terraces and left them as litter. They were not standards to be carried into battle. The game was over and they went home and turned their back on us again.

The bottle-throwing and the insults before and during the game were part of the pantomime that is match day in Turin. They make those throat-cutting gestures to everyone and this is what we had lived in terror of, the stuff of nightmares.

I had arrived in Turin with a heavy baggage of fear, expecting retribution – however misplaced - to be taken. Walking the streets, there was a sense that, at any moment, someone would drive a knife into your back. That they would pick out your big, red Scouse face in a narrow street and make you pay for Brussels. It was all paranoia. They were just contemptuously indifferent. They have learnt to live with Heysel. They just did not want to live with us.

Carrying so much fear, Liverpool fans could have behaved in the manner English supporters normally adopt, facing their worries with bluster and colonising Turin's squares. Instead, sanity reigned. Most stayed out of the city and those who did go in left the banners and singing for the stadium. They behaved - except for the handful of halfwits who made collapsing-wall gestures - with restraint and decorum. Had they misbehaved in the city, it might have forced the locals out of indifference and blood would have been spilt. We could leave with pride in more than the result.

The police did a good job, too, with a light touch that came as a surprise for seasoned European travellers. As Liverpool fans dispersed all over northern Italy, just one coach headed back to Turin city centre. It was escorted by eight police vans – man-to-man marking and a sweeper system taken to the extreme.

In the centre, Turin was silent, the only sign of life a small group of *drughi* near the station. They didn't really want trouble, either. Like the hooligan groups at home, they wanted to make a show of strength and feel lawless. But their *drughi* T-shirts handily tipped off the police, making confrontation almost impossible.

Turin handled Liverpool's visit better than anyone could have imagined. It looked like a lovely city. God, I hope I never have to go back.

12

Coming up the hill

IT'S GETTING NEAR the end of extra time. The mental anguish of two hours is reaching its climax. We've hit emotional depths, been lifted to unimagined heights and… fallen back on stock phrases. The game we have witnessed has scrambled coherent thought and everyone seems to be communicating in the formulaic phrases of the game. 'It's all about heart now,' one man said to no one. 'It's who wants it most'. Some don't even speak, just cram their fists into their mouths and gnaw, knowing that in 10 minutes it will all be over. The final whistle sounds and someone says: 'It's a lottery.' There's a big rush towards the toilets. 'Twitchy bum time,' the king of the cliché says. Indeed.

As Istanbul got nearer, Dave was increasingly erratic. I sent him to the cash machine to get money on my card while I watched the bags and he came back with a single note. 'Is that enough?' I asked, knowing that we needed provisions for the journey.

'I think so, I got confused,' he said. 'We don't need much, anyway. We'll never be able to change it back.'

So he went to a mini-supermarket and arrived back looking sheepish, short on beer, cheese and meat. 'I didn't think I'd have enough,' he said, explaining.

'Well get more money out.'

'But I've made a mistake. The girl gave me this in change.'

He held out a wad of notes. A real wad. Thick and showoffy, like a Chelsea fan's up north.

'You've got hundreds of quid out on my card! I'll never be able to change it back! You're an idiot.'

'I got confused.' Not with your own card earlier, I thought. Just mine.

'Go and get enough food. And get me a beer before you go.'

Bucharest was suddenly proving expensive. I managed to get on to the internet using the laptop and mobile while he was gone and checked the exchange rates. The wad he had left me was worth £16. Keep quiet about that, I thought.

We drank another beer and I kept shaking my head at him. There were others, doing the same, and some obvious expressions of disgust from passers-by.

Dave had one hand thrust deep into his hip pocket. It was moving in a way that scares nuns and spinsters. His fingers jiggled around, touching something for comfort - his ticket. It was secreted close to the area of his body that he unconsciously protects most. A young woman tutted as if he was making some sort of advance, but it was the farthest thing from his mind. He just needed to feel that ticket. It's compulsive. So that's why he'd been sleeping in his jeans.

But Dave's game of finger-wiggly was tame compared to the vista as the train pulled out of the station. Police were patrolling the trackside for some 400 yards, but after that the sidings deteriorated into a mini shanty town. A man was squatting beside a large cardboard box – the sort a cooker is delivered in – defecating on the ground. He was gnarled and wiry like an American mountain man and waved at us to look away in aggressive defiance, as if we were peeking through his bathroom window. We were, I suppose.

It does not take much insight to feel that you are going backwards on the journey from Bucharest through Bulgaria. Every train station looks as if it had been shelled at some point in the previous week and the people appear to have battle fatigue. To them, it must have looked like we were riding in glorious luxury.

Even a relatively pampered journey like this puts things in perspective. Shortly after leaving Bucharest, I visited the bathroom. There was no shower, just two inches of broken cable that spewed cold water when the tap was turned. While the washing area was clean, I squatted under this makeshift shower and felt a pure pleasure from rinsing my body. The cleanliness didn't last. Back in the compartment I could feel the sweat pores opening again. They oozed liquid but also picked up the dense flavours of the carriage. Within minutes you suck in the pall of cigarettes and sweat and blend in perfectly with the background like an olfactory chameleon.

The landscape was riven by steep, verdant gorges, sliding down to huge disused factories that look like they were the object of a quarrel between armies in Stalingrad. They ran for hundreds of yards alongside the track. Where the workers employed here during the Communist era were housed is anyone's guess. Underground, to judge by the lack of obvious dwelling places. These countries look like they have been plundered over and over again – probably because they have. A new, vicious round of exploitation appears to be in motion as the state monopolies of the past fracture and find their way into private hands. In the rush to capitalism, no provision seems to have been made for the people of these valleys. Those who have energy and intelligence will leave, only to be derided as asylum seekers and illegal immigrants when they pitch up in western Europe. The most vocal of their critics are always the first to advise the dispossessed to get on their bikes. The profits created by the new market economies in the east are always welcome in the cities of the west; their (human) losses no one wants.

The routine of border checks was a welcome distraction, though there is only so far a bleeding heart can go. The Bulgarian passport inspector appeared with an armful of Liverpool memorabilia. 'You English? Go to Istanbul?' he asked menacingly. 'You give me something for my son. You rich. We poor. I want something.' This was delivered in enough of a Slavic growl to suggest quite a bit of the sweat that infuses these carriages was delivered cold. Here, though, he had picked the wrong pair.

'Got nothin', mate.'

'You give,' he threatened

'You piss off.' And he did. It was easy to see how this man supplemented his income with a little bullying.

We slept fitfully until the three-hour saga that is entering Turkey began. The Bulgarians here were not acquisitive, but it was three in the morning, so perhaps it was hard for them to summon the energy. Across the border at Svilengrad, they did not expend any. For the first time we had to get off the train and take our passports to the Turks.

'*Midnight Express*,' Dave said as we climbed across the tracks and joined a long queue. There were another half-dozen Liverpool supporters waiting nervously. Some tried to show camaraderie, but it was a tense atmosphere. The pressure rose considerably when a very grumpy official demanded that we stand against a wall and shouted: 'I want tickets.' And it was clear that he did not mean a Balkan five-day railpass. I felt like saying: 'So do I, you officious tosspot.'

Slowly, nervously, the precious tickets were produced. The Turk collected and stacked them, leaving them sitting on a counter while the rest of the passengers were dealt with. There was nervous laughter and then a gasp. The official picked up the pile and disappeared into another room with the match tickets.

Dave had to bite his tongue, which, given the *Midnight Express* thoughtline he'd been ploughing, should have come as a relief for the border guard. He looked ready to explode ... until the passport and ticket reappeared. The price of the visa to enter Turkey was included in the match ticket and a special stamp was required. However, Dave would gladly pay the £10 entry fee to put the years back on his life.

'I nearly lost it when he went with the ticket,' he said as we got back on the train to wait for customs and the police. 'And when he came back and called my name, I thought we were going to end up in the Goulash.'

Well, it would have been better than the Gulag, but surely worse than the soup. All we needed to do now was sleep for four hours and we would be in Istanbul.

PART FOUR

13

To glory we will go

BOTH SIDES ARE milling around on the pitch, deciding which players have the nerve to take part in a shootout that could earn them a place in their club's history or haunt them for their entire career – perhaps the rest of their life. Carragher chases down Dudek and manhandles him, shouting and gesturing like an ejected drunk. He's the most excitable person in the stadium. Everyone else is too nervous to expend energy.

The penalties are at the Milan end and they go first. Serginho steps up to take the first kick. He places the ball on the spot and walks back. As he turns, Dudek starts to dance on the line. It's 1984 again. Carragher's a genius. He's proven that history does matter.

Another station, another nation, another taxi tout. At 8.30 on Monday morning, we're finally walking along the platform at Istanbul. The journey that began on Thursday night at Lime Street is over but the only thought was to shrug off the persistent hustler who shadowed me for about 30 yards despite being told that I was not interested. He was huge, so I suspected he was trying a bit of intimidation.

'I've told you, mate, don't need it. Now f…'

Dave rushed up beside me just as the man put his hand on my shoulder.

'Are you blind?'

I must have been, because it was Big Al. So the first reunion of the day began, with more than a touch of embarrassment.

Al arrived from Sydney on Saturday and had either taken up trainspotting or been checking every arrival for two days. He was aware that we were arriving by rail, but unsure when. As usual, we adjourn to the nearest bar to the station and settle down to catch up. We had hardly taken a sip of the breakfast Efes when Mark strolled past with a mate in search of an early morning kebab. It was like some kind of demented school reunion. He hadn't seen Al for 15 years. 'Alright mate,' he said. And then: 'Were you OK in Turin? You went back into town, didn't you?'

'It was a doddle,' I said, using the idiom of the 1980s.

With the exception of Dave, who is younger, we all go back that far and more. In the late 1970s, disorder on the streets and football had become forever linked. Travel to away matches had begun to be policed like military operations, with supporters herded on to 'special' trains, made up of the oldest rolling stock. They were the sort of carriages that would not be missed if a bunch of thugs decided to wreck their own transport. Destroying trains always sounded a crazy idea to us; after all, you had to have some way of getting home.

Special trains had the lowest standards of service humanly possible. Football followers tend to attract that kind of treatment, because the vendors know that they will come back for more no matter how brutalised they are. Police watched the fans embark at their home station, marshalled them at the other end into what we called 'the escort', marched the entire trainload to the ground and then locked everyone in after the game before reversing the process for the homeward journey. There was no buffet and no opportunity to stop for food and drink. Worse were the omnipotent powers of arrest for the police.

Yet many supporters believed that this was the only way to keep safe from attack by rival fans when off their own turf. Al and I reacted against this by taking the normal, scheduled trains. These were commonly referred to in Liverpool as 'ordinary' trains, to distinguish them from 'the specials'.

'Ordinary boys' were not a gang, in the sense the ICFs and the Service Crews touted themselves. It was a loose collection of small groups who took this method of transport for a variety of reasons. Most just wanted a drink and timed their arrival in cities across the country for pub opening hours. Others liked to pay for their adventures with a little pre-match shoplifting. A few, very few, liked to play at being hooligans.

If you left Lime Street early enough, the police would not be in place at the destination. It meant that if there were any local troublemakers waiting you were vulnerable. In practice it rarely happened. The main danger was after the match, but even that was overstated.

Most of the time it was easy to find a quiet pub. By about 7pm both police and locals had drifted home to get ready for Saturday night and the stations were quiet places again and homeward embarkation easy.

Taking the ordinary gave you a certain glamour. The specials might arrive back at, say, seven o'clock and we'd swagger into the Yankee at nine-thirty to the breathless question: 'Any trouble.'

'Nah, it was a doddle.'

Ordinary boys were the elite, the risk-takers. People listened to your itinerary with awe. 'Youse're mad, youse are,' they'd say. And cool. You could hear it in their voices.

It was important to look the part, too. The whole 'casual' culture was beginning to be noticed in the media but things had moved on in Liverpool by the time that journalists noticed any trends. The development of the terrace 'look' was originally an accident. Near where I lived, off Scotland Road, was a Salvation Army hostel used by the homeless and long-distance lorry drivers. The truckers parked in the wastelands levelled during the building of the second Mersey tunnel. There, local boys would attempt to break into the lorries. Some time in 1976, a consignment of Fred Perry polo shirts was stolen.

Within days, everyone was wearing Fred Perrys. Bought at a fraction of the retail price, they were very popular.

So when Liverpool supporters went to the Continent on the pre-season tours or for European Cup games, some paid for the trip with a little shoplifting. They stole what they knew was easily shifted back home. In early 1978, Lacoste polo shirts started showing up in Liverpool, presumably because they were the nearest thing in Europe to Fred Perrys.

The Mod revival at the end of the 1970s mutated into a style popular with football fans. The suede boots of the Mod era were as common as training shoes on the ordinaries and, by 1980, the look was well established. Lacoste, Lois or Lee jeans, Hush Puppies or adidas samba. As soon as the London mobs started to adopt the style, we junked it.

By 1982, we were avoiding labels. John Smedley botany wool crew necks – the new target for shoplifters – were expensive but unlabelled. Some of us were getting Levi 501s sent over from the States, shrinking them and bleaching them. At Euston Station, West Ham fans waiting for a train north had their eyes on stalks as we came off the ordinary mob-handed in faded jeans. They were too shocked to cause any trouble. A couple of weeks later, when we visited Upton Park, it was clear there had been a run on bleach in the East End.

Then we stopped. The style had nowhere to go. We left the chase for a new designer shirt or jeans to others. The 'scally' look stayed understated as labels predominated. That said, we would always admire a classy pair of training shoes. In 1982, Manchester United fans came into the Kop and there was serious trouble. The topic of conversation after the game was the high-profile arrest of a lad we knew. He'd been dragged out of the Kop with a policeman on each limb, flailing away in a manic and futile attempt to escape.

In the Yankee, Al was effusive in his admiration. 'Did you see Wayne?' he asked. 'He had a lovely pair of Forrest Hills on.' The trainers had caught the eye, even if the method of displaying them left something to desired.

Tasty trainers drew envy but, for the most part, we'd rather wear a quality pair of suede boots, preferably purchased at half the price they were marked up in the Jermyn Street shop that the boys visited. On the ordinaries, style mattered, not fashion.

So we were ordinary boys and proud of it. Status comes in many different ways and the subversion of the language was entirely in keeping with the culture we lived in, whose values clashed with the mores of British life.

It was a culture that flirted with lawlessness but, for us, never came near to drifting into criminality. We always thought Mark was living wilder than we were; it would not surprise me if he thought we were nearer the edge.

Mark and his mates had been to Istanbul before, when Liverpool played Galatasaray. He gushed about the place, saying that we would have a wonderful time. There was some concern at home that this was the city where two Leeds United supporters were stabbed to death in 2001.

'Don't know what that was all about, but I think those boys were probably unlucky,' Mark said. 'They're friendly here. The Turks were great with us.'

'Have you been the Blue Mosque?' I asked. Mark was appalled.

'I'm going nowhere blue,' he said with conviction. 'The world's all red.' It was and it felt good. The boys were gathering again and it was for the European Cup.

Then Mark was off. Like Al, he has lived away from Liverpool for a long time. Yet even if they get to fewer matches than they once did, the football club is the mooring line that keeps people like Mark and Al close to their identity. Their sense of self is tied up with a red shirt, a Liver Bird and the songs and experiences that have bound us together since we were barely in our teens.

The sun was out, the Turkish people friendly and things could not have been better. It was an auspicious start to four days in Turkey.

Without the aid of a street map and on the basis of a confused barman's directions, we headed uphill to the hotel and immediately got lost. Of course, a taxi would have been less time-consuming but blundering into people and places is an integral part of the experience. Had we gone straight to the hotel, for example, we would never have met Bill.

We were standing on a corner, each having favoured heading towards a different compass point, when a portly Turk accosted us. We had already noticed that the local guidance industry was a competitive business and the more successful operators had an obvious mixture of charm, threat and knowledge. Bill came up short on all fronts, which probably explained why he was forced to try his luck with an unpleasant looking trio like us when there were clearly more affluent and pliable tourists in the area.

Bill's grasp of English caused problems. There was always going to be a basic cultural misunderstanding between us. That's because he spoke the language better than we did. He had an idiomatic form of expression that suggested he had once been a scripwriter on *Minder*. His physique and face could have seen him cast as a comic but violent villain. He was short, fat and had an impressive scar running down his cheek. I could see Al liked him immediately and presumed he'd be with us for the long haul.

'Where are you going? Let me see. Like a rabbit warren round here. Come on, this way. You have to be careful. Tea leaves everywhere.'

He didn't need to tell us that. Most of them we knew from home.

Bill's real name was incomprehensible but he was proud of his anglicised nickname. He led us around a variety of shops and bars owned by acquaintances and family members. 'Ah, it's the Bill,' a waiter said. Whenever cash was exchanged, he went off unabashed to haggle for his share. 'I'll just divvy up with them,' Bill said as he sloped off to get his portion of our largesse from the owner of the business. 'Cor blimey, this is alright,' he'd gloat, proudly showing us the euros he had earned.

In bars, Bill was on safe ground. He ordered food for us with an aristocratic flourish and called for drink with the abandon of a man who never has to pay. He was less certain when the questions stretched further than catering.

Near the Blue Mosque, a hawker with a stall was wearing a fez. Publicity at home had suggested wearing such a hat was a mortal insult to Turks. 'Why don't people wear the fez, Bill?'

'Ataturk didn't like them.'

'Why?' Bill thought for a full 30 seconds and shrugged. 'Everybody love Ataturk.'

'Then why's he wearing one?' Al asked, pointing at the stallholder.

The question seriously taxed Bill. The delay was much longer this time. Finally, he replied. 'Because he's a c***!' he roared.

Throughout the day, our group grew and shrunk as friends, people we vaguely recognised and even complete strangers arrived and departed. When someone told us he was in transit between the Blue Mosque and the New Mosque, Dave sighed. 'So many mosques, so little time,' he said. On the face of it, Homer Simpson could not have expressed with any more precision the sense of living in a cultural void.

But we had filled that void. The Scouse diaspora had come together and the venue was incidental. For all they – we – cared, the Golden Horn was a dubious nightclub and the Spice Bazaar an unlikely Geri Halliwell comeback. That's because we were there for business. Leave tourism to the tourists. Byzantium, Constantinople, Istanbul... the city had been here a long time. It will still be here when we want to see it properly. As it was, it felt like the Ottoman Empire was in bloom the last time we won the European Cup.

Going to football matches abroad is unlike any other type of travel. The destination is the least important thing in the whole adventure. Tickets, trophies and gathering with people with the same values and experiences are the only things that matter.

To suggest it was just Scousers arriving for the game, though, would be to underestimate the level of support for Liverpool. People had come from the Far East, all over northern Europe and the Americas. We met a young Dubliner alone at a bus stop and invited him to drink with us. Bill had promised to take us to a special bar, his favourite. There was high expectation.

It turned out to be the place that we had visited nine hours earlier when we first left the train station. The barman recognised us but did not seem to know Bill. Our guide was despondent as we bantered away. The young Irishman sat agape at sectarian insults that flew across the table. Al called us 'dirty Taigs', while he was immediately derided as an 'Orange bastard' in response.

'You've shocked the bogman,' Dave said when he noticed the lad's expression.

'I can't believe it,' the Dubliner said. 'You're English.' He clearly thought we were putting on a show on his behalf.

It was time for a little history lesson. 'Where I come from,' I said, 'we had an Irish Nationalist MP until 1929. So I won't be called English by a Free Stater. I'm Scouse. Not only that. Go to O'Connoll Street when you get home and look at the statues: Jimmy Larkin with his arms wide open, one of Ireland's great heroes. Well, he's Scouse.'

Even if he didn't get into the game, this boy would take a few stories back to Ireland. What he could not understand is that the residue of the religious divide remains in Liverpool, but is mostly confined to idle insults. The football clubs have done much to help bridge the divides, drawing support from both sides. There is still the capacity for religious unrest on the Celtic fringe of the northwest, but it is very small. That we have grown up together merrily slinging sectarian insults around is probably the best sign that the communities are at ease with each other.

Unfortunately for Bill, he was now really out of his depth. Running out of material, he tried a little intimidation.

'You don't fuck with me. I'm a killer,' he said.

Al, all six-and-a-half feet of him, put him in his place: 'Yeah, you're killing time drinking our ale.'

Bill made a last attempt to impress us. 'You can have anything, the lot. I can get you anything you want in Istanbul,' he said. There must have been ten of us around the table and only three had tickets. OK Bill, that's what we want.

'No bloody chance,' he said sadly. 'Big cash. Big cash. And I'm not getting it.' He looked disappointed. A silence fell on the bar. When even the Bill can't get paid, it looked like it would be a tough day for the ticketless on Wednesday.

Yet it was hard to be too gloomy. Outside we could hear the call to prayer. Just. It was drowned out by Liverpool fans repeatedly parroting the trumpet line from Johnny Cash's *Ring of Fire*. It would be a long, long night.

14

With a Liver bird upon my chest

I T GOES OVER THE bar. For a moment the place goes wild but the comedown is rapid. Serginho, looking shattered, crosses paths with Hamann and the uncrossed fingers squirm against each other again. It's a great position to be in, but Stevie Nicol missed the first one in 1984. It's not over yet.

Hamann, cool, slots it in. For the first time all night, we're in the lead…

As usual, Al was up too early and looked too fresh. He woke us arriving at the hotel with his bag. He was only able to find a place to stay until Monday night and he surveyed his home for the next two nights with distaste. There was only a double bed for the three of us.

I noticed that Dave had slept in his underpants. Either he was so drunk he didn't care about the ticket – unlikely – or he has hidden it in a place so secure he can relax.

We discussed the night's activities. We left Al with Bill and the rest about 7.30 to clean up. We had a loose arrangement to meet near Taksim Square later but it never happened. Our night deteriorated into a drunken reiteration of those things we are here for – love, belief, culture – while we gorged on red meat and a westernised belly dancer vibrated, ignored, in the background. Al went through the same process, but he was not sure where, and with whom.

Outside, the streets were filling up with Liverpool supporters. And things were turning ugly. 'Christ,' I said to Dave. 'We have a seriously hideous-looking mob.' It was all aleguts and shaven heads, enhanced by overtight T-shirts and shorts.

'I know,' he said. 'I was down the Strand last week. I looked around and felt like Brad Pitt.'

I hoped it was rhyming slang. The Strand is the shopping centre in Bootle that achieved notoriety as the place where Jamie Bulger, the two-year-old, was abducted by two other children before being brutally murdered. It has certainly seen ugliness.

The few Milan supporters we saw were clearly worried. They were undoubtedly the safest football fans in the world. They just didn't know it. Our history meant that there would have to be serious provocation for anyone to get involved in trouble with opposing supporters. The Italians moved warily around the tourist sites but did not seem to venture into the bars – at least not the sort we drank in.

And the drinking holes were filling up fast as more and more Liverpool supporters flooded into the city. By noon they were already boisterous, some dancing like Pinocchio having a seizure to the ubiquitous riff from *Ring of Fire*. There were two options: join a group we knew and risk humiliation and hangover – to be filmed on someone's video doing an epileptic jig under the influence would be too much to bear – or take to the water. Down on the Galata Bridge, we mulled over the possibilities with a beer.

It was unanimous. We must go to Asia. We'd seen people we knew the previous day and asked them what they'd done. 'Been to Asia,' one said casually. 'Bit like going to Birkenhead, only more civilised. Oh, and bigger, we've heard. But we didn't get to see it all.' It sounded good to us.

We chose the most rickety boat available, for no other reason than stupid bravado. 'Let's pick the one most likely to go down.' Beside the vessel, the locals were having lunch. A stallholder was grilling fish with his back to the water, extracting the bones with a flourish from the cooked flesh and throwing them back into the Bosporus. The fillet, pushed into a bread roll, looked delicious. 'That's what I'm having for dinner,' I said. 'With your bowels?' the other two choroused. With three of us in one tiny room, this was becoming an issue.

From Vienna onwards, things had got worse. A diet of red meat, beer and a tendency to favour gutterside home cooking had caused a number of panicky moments, if no disasters. Street vendors are probably the wrong choice for someone already suffering raw jaxy syndrome but the smells, the tastes... they are tempting, especially after a gallon of Efes.

The other thing is that I was unused to beer. Well, crap beer at least. The carbonated, coloured and alcoholic water served across Eastern Europe and Turkey was truly awful, but drinking is such an integral part of the experience that sacrifices had to be made.

'I wish the final was somewhere where they had good beer,' I said, sadly, grimacing at yet another glass of chemical fizz while looking across the Bosporus. 'Somewhere like Brussels.'

'You like to rephrase that?'

'On reflection, I'm happy here.'

Afloat, we were impressed by the sights to a greater or lesser degree. Inonu Stadium, home to Besiktas, drew admiring coos both for its design and its location beside the water. The Dolmabahce Palace got less rave reviews.

By the time we reached land, Al and Dave were desperate to have a beer on Asian soil. I was just desperate. We had 20 minutes to achieve our objectives.

Even before the drinks were ordered, I made a rush for the toilet. Not good. They had finished their beer by the time I got back and had ordered a second. But time was not the only thing running out. Sure enough, the ship had sailed before I was comfortable enough to make the walk back to the quay.

The bridge spanning two continents was not far away so we hiked up its slip road aiming to stroll back to Europe. The idea of walking from

one continent to another appealed to us. Unfortunately, a traffic policeman would not let us pass and sent us back. Luckily, there was a bus
picking up at a stop so we piled on. Where it was going, we had no idea,
except to Europe. That was part of the fun.

As it happened, it was hell. After about 15 minutes, we arrived outside the Ali Sami Yen Stadium, famous for its 'Welcome to hell' image
earned when Manchester United received a ferocious reception there.
Well, any enemies of United are friends of ours, so we jumped off the
bus and went into the ground, which was being demolished at one end,
to pay homage to Galatasaray.

In Britain, a site manager, or one of the workmen, would shoo any
interlopers away from a hard-hat area where bricks and debris are flying. Here, the labourers did not even have protective headgear and did-
n't give three inquisitive Scousers a second look. The banners from the
last game to take place here were still hanging and we thought about
taking a souvenir, but it felt a little like graverobbing.

Well, enough of the historic sights. Now for Taksim Square and the
countdown to the game.

* * *

Behaviour is all about perception. We arrived at the square about 8.30 and
there was bedlam. Now, there are two ways of interpreting the sight that
played out in front of us. There is the 1980s view: mobs of drunks block-
ing the roads, drunkenly accosting innocent citizens, causing damage to
property, putting themselves at risk and urinating and vomiting in public.

The opposite inference? A good-natured, exuberant group, enjoying
a big party and inviting everyone in the vicinity to join them.
Thankfully, the Turkish police chose the latter view of the situation, but
less excitable crowds than this have drawn baton charges and tear gas in
the past.

Thousands of Liverpool fans had colonised one corner of the square
and swarmed over a row of low-rise kiosk-style shops. Hundreds were

bouncing on the flat roofs, to the delight of the hordes below. Banners obscured the shop signs and beer was being splashed up and down like a perverse water fight. Everyone was singing 'Rafa, Rafa Benitez…' to the tune of *La Bamba* and any suggestion of a silence was greeted with *Ring of Fire.*

Some 30ft up a tree, a fan, obviously drunk, was hugging the bark tight. His friends – and plenty of enemies, by the look of it – were shaking the trunk, so that the tree was swaying across an arc of 60 degrees. It almost seemed that the plant would be ripped from its roots. When the crowd focused on what was happening, they chanted: 'Shake the monkey, shake the monkey…'

It was time to find somewhere a little less rowdy and we took to the backstreets, pausing briefly to contemplate the area in front of the Burger King where the Leeds fans were stabbed. There was no hint of tension, but it was a sobering thought in a sober-free zone.

Surprisingly, the alleyways around the square were quiet, with only a few Liverpool supporters dotted around. It was a good place to eat and get set for an early night. I vowed to leave at midnight. Tomorrow, after all, was a big day. The others wanted to stay.

Unfortunately, just as midnight was about to strike, someone suggested that Michel Platini was a greater player than Zinedine Zidane. It was impossible to walk away and ignore an assertion like that, even if I had my heart set on sleep. To let ignorance reign, without rebuke, is moral cowardice of the highest order. So we ordered more alcohol – well, we'd been meaning to try the raki all night – and began to debate the issue. Four hours later, I believed I'd made the point forcefully enough to win the argument. At least when I went to sleep I knew I'd done something worthwhile that day.

There was just one other ugly incident that occurred before the night ended. The taxi driver got lost in the old town and we drove in circles. Sitting in the front seat, I could not see what happened, but Dave gave out a loud snore, which could have been mistaken for a snort of ecstasy.

Turning around, I saw that Al was also asleep – with his face nuzzled in to Dave's groin area. It was horrible. The only thing to do was to wake them up with a stream of abuse that cast doubt on their sexuality. I was satisfied to see that Al had dribbled in his sleep, or at least, I told them both, that was the spin they could put on it in the morning.

They were indignant, confused and unable to respond with any coherent strategy. This tale will resurface to humiliate them all the way to the next European Cup final, even if it takes another 20 years.

Everything had turned out perfectly and the driver received an extravagant tip for the bounty his ineptitude provided. The one blot on the horizon – where the sun had now risen – was that I still had not got a ticket. I went to sleep wondering who hates *Ring of Fire* more: me or the *muezzins*. It was already match day – May 25. An auspicious date. It was 28 years to the day since we first won the European Cup.

15

Smiles and joy and glee

ANDREA PIRLO IS UP next. To judge by his walk, he's nervous. Dudek is calmer on the line, as if embarrassed by his previous antics. Pirlo hits it to his left, the goalkeeper goes the right way and the ball has neither the power nor the direction to go in. Djibril Cisse saunters into the spotlight. You can see from his extreme haircuts that he has a confidence that his ability probably does not warrant. But he has no fear and while the ball might end up among the Milan fans, he won't lose his nerve on the run-up as so often happens in these situations. He doesn't. Two-nil. You can almost touch the cup…

'Morning lovers.' They both turned away, recalling the horror of accidental drunken contact misinterpreted.

'Show us your ticket,' Dave hit back.

'Below the belt. But you know all about that, don't you.' Yes, the level of repartee was that sad.

Between the three of us, we had travelled 11,000 miles and taken 18 days just to get here. And the reason we came – or at least its physical manifestation – would take place within 12 hours. But first there was a commitment I wished I hadn't made. A car was picking me up in 30 minutes to take part in a live Turkish television programme. Dave was coming along for the ride, the idea being to have a panel of fans from both sides. Al was hanging around to make contact with the rest of our mates.

I had intended to get a shirt washed and ironed to look vaguely respectable for the cameras. Drink and banter, as so often happens, got between good intentions and reality.

Wearing a polo shirt and having a week's worth of stubble was not the greatest look for an apparent representative of the paper of record, but that was never part of my plan. If it was, I would have been comfortable in the press box for the match. Instead, the level of discomfort was acute. Facing the cameras was bad enough; the prospect of watching the game on television was really moving the sweat glands along. People asked me why I never applied for press credentials or tried to climb on to the corporate junket bandwagon, but the reasons are simple. No matter how you become involved in football, whether or not it becomes your livelihood, it is crucial not to lose sight of the pure, simple truths that draw you to the game. I was there as a fan and the press box is for people who are working. As for corporate hospitality, I'd rather be locked out of the ground or watching on television. It would compromise my sense of self to be part of that rarefied, privileged group rather than in the rough-and-tumble world of the footsoldier supporters. Plus, no one offered me the opportunity, the bastards.

That morning, I was regretting the press box highmindedness and would have shared canapés and supped with a red devil to get into that bloody Ataturk stadium.

A rather tall, elegant girl at the television company seemed reluctant to believe that I was the man they expected. One of the production crew came to the rescue and took us into the green room where we tried to rehydrate. The other British journalist was Patrick Barclay, from the *Sunday Telegraph*. He breezed in – thank heavens – in a T-shirt and jeans. However, there was one difference: I looked scruffy and he looked the epitome of cool.

Our Italian counterparts stared at us askance. They had dressed for the occasion. The woman must have been expecting to go to a P2 Masonic lodge ladies' night, while her male colleague was clearly off to become a 'made man' with one of the five families the minute the cameras stopped rolling.

Dave could hardly contain himself. 'He's a Corleone. You haven't got a chance. He made his bones when you were dating cheerleaders. Did you see him shooting his cuffs?'

The host did more talking than his guests and then we were off, back to the hotel. The less time on camera the better, I felt. In the car, there was a text message: 'S has a 100 euro ticket. U want it?'

Oh yes.

* * *

At the hotel, there was a crucial moment. A decision loomed: what to wear for the match? I took from my bag a one-off T-shirt made by Kevin, my cousin, a man of almost too many talents. It was white with a red rectangle running down the solar plexus. That oblong contains a picture of Bill Shankly holding his clenched fist high with a look of determination on his face. It was more than 25 years since I had worn any sort of colours at a match. I put the T-shirt on. Tonight, it would be time to stand up and be counted.

* * *

Without Shankly, would we be in Istanbul? That question does not refer to the club he rebuilt after taking over as manager on December 1, 1959. Nor is it meant to assess the teams he created. It is about the metaphysical effect that he had on the supporters, the sense of involvement, belief and love he fostered. Ian St John, the man who scored the goal that brought the FA Cup back to Anfield for the first time in 1965, said: 'For Bill Shankly, football was a moral issue rather than mere sport.' Shankly communicated this to the supporters and made them believe the game was – is – about bigger matters.

He was a socialist who had an unerring faith in people, a man with exceptional powers of motivation and he made us understand that this football club was more than just a business. More than anyone, he made it a cultural symbol.

It was a stunning synthesis. Shankly was a natural demagogue who had found a constituency whose tastes tramlined perfectly with his vision. That he built a successful team very quickly was almost secondary; his appeal transcended the mere kicking of a ball. The statue that stands outside the Kop shows him with his arms outstretched, taking the acclaim, fists clenched and has the legend 'He made the people happy' on its plinth. Shankly did. He also charged the supporters with a fervour that went sometimes beyond the bounds of rationality and fed a belief that this game could become a vehicle for a people's hopes and dreams; that success in football could become a weapon in the guerrilla warfare that a downtrodden and alienated section of society was constantly conducting in a world that ignored their interests and aspirations.

After the club got rid of him in an unseemly manner in 1974 – a compulsive resigner, he did it once too often and they jumped at the chance – he went to games at Anfield and Goodison for pleasure. One night, coming out of an Everton home match – in the days when it was cheap, most football-mad youngsters went to both grounds in the city – I saw Shankly appear from the players' entrance. The crowd waiting for autographs milled around him and followed him down the road as he began the three-mile walk home. People asked questions and he answered them, his love of the game showing in his enthusiasm. Over the journey, some dropped off, so that the group of about 80 was down to 20 or so by the time he reached home. At his gate – outside a humble semi in West Derby – he said: 'I'd love to invite you in, boys, but I'd be in trouble with the missus…' He pulled a henpecked face. Magnificent. It was a very long walk home, but worth it.

Shankly's most famous axiom, however, has been used against Liverpool supporters. 'Football is not a matter of life and death,' he is quoted as saying. 'It's much more important than that.'

After Heysel and Hillsborough, this statement has been used to illustrate Liverpool supporters' loss of perspective when it comes to the sport. It is unfair. The comment originally came out of a press conference, when Shankly was devastated that his side had been beaten. 'Come on Bill,' a journalist asked. 'It's not a matter of life or death, is it?'

'It's much more serious than that,' he shot back. He may have been an Ayrshire miner but, like Scousers, he could not resist the easy joke. Then, when he saw the effect that the comment had – people were appalled and amused in equal measure – he turned it into his party piece. But do not be fooled. He knew what really mattered. And he is the guiding light for people like us, whose perception of what the game means diverges wildly from the beliefs of the men in the boardrooms.

And we know, more than most, exactly how important football is.

* * *

How much would defeat in Istanbul hurt? To be honest, quite a lot. But not that much. At the end of the 1989 season, when Arsenal scored the last-minute goal at Anfield to snatch the title and the Double from Liverpool's grasp, there was shock on the Kop. Then a voice spoke up somewhere behind where we stood. 'Worse things happen,' it said. 'We know.' And we laughed at the absurdity of being left distraught by defeat.

The eight of us who gathered at a cafe table near the New Mosque knew that. There was me, Dave and Big Al, Ian and Stephen, whose dad had been so horribly stabbed in Rome, Stevie, Pat and Tony, whose brother John had been beaten in Brussels for his pigeon Italian. Defeat by Milan would be disappointing and irritating. But it would be no nightmare. We had all suffered real ones... Rome, Heysel, Hillsborough. All of us had been at Hillsborough.

* * *

April 15, 1989 was such a lovely spring day. While waiting for our lift to Sheffield, my brother said that he hoped the traffic would not be so bad. My response was: 'What can possibly go wrong on a beautiful day like this?'

Tony was living in London but met two carloads of us at a pub. He had not been at Heysel when his brother was jumped by Scousers but he chuckled about the incident with the rest of us. No one would laugh at what happened to Tony at Hillsborough.

He was with me, the two of us lingering in the pub for a final drink while the rest of the party drifted down to the ground. We headed for the Leppings Lane at about 2.45.

When we got to the gates, the queues were backed up into the street. It was not a particularly bad crush though and, being experienced in crowds, we were able to surf the pushing and shoving and make our way to the front.

As we reached the turnstiles, the main, exit gate opened. We were surprised. In front of us was the tunnel that led to the central section of the terraces. People ran towards it. I was in the stands, so I went off to the side. Tony went straight ahead. I next saw him 32 hours later. Life had changed considerably in that short time.

There was no hint of potential problems before the gate opened and let the crowds in shortly before kick-off. Even then, I went to my seat without any worries. I emerged into the stand just as the teams came out. It was just a joy to be there. Nottingham Forest, in all white, and Liverpool, glorious in blood red ran onto a pitch that looked lush and perfect in the sunlight.

The first feelings of alarm occurred as I moved towards the goal-line heading for my seat. The Leppings Lane end comprised a number of separate pens. The subway that Tony had moved towards led to the central terrace, directly behind the goal. That area was too packed. The wings of the terrace had large empty areas that should have been full of people. It did not take an expert to see that something had gone wrong.

This was a semi-final and many of the people present that day did not know the geography of the stadium. For plenty of fans in Hillsborough, this would be the only time in the season that they would watch Liverpool away from Anfield – unless, of course, the team reached the final. Emerging from the turnstiles, the only apparent entrance to the terraces was the subway. Those who had been to the ground regularly knew that a short walk left or right of the subway would bring you round and allow entry into the other sections behind the goal. Too few people that day were aware of this. A single policeman stationed at that one visible entrance, directing people to the side, could have saved 96 lives.

We also did not know that at a semi-final between Tottenham Hotspur and Wolverhampton Wanderers in 1981 a dangerous crush had happened in the same place in similar circumstances.

By the time the game kicked off, there were clearly problems behind the goal. The police, fixated on potential hooliganism, did not act and actively pushed people back into danger when they attempted to climb out and onto the pitch. When Peter Beardsley hit the bar at the Kop end after four minutes, it was the final straw. There were serious problems at the Leppings Lane.

Now I started to worry for my youngest brother. He had left us about 1.15 and we had reminded him to go to the side. A raised section to the goal's left had the best views in the end and we had told him to go there.

Soon, the extent of the nightmare began to show itself. A man walked along the sidelines holding his elbow in his hand. The elbow made a right-angle; halfway up the forearm, there was another right-angle.

Within minutes a fat man was laid down on the pitch in front of us, with people pumping at his chest. So much was going on that I looked away for a minute. When I checked again, his huge belly was exposed because his red shirt had been pulled up to cover his face. 'Christ, he's dead,' I exclaimed. It was involuntary, the product of shock.

Those around me, however, turned nasty. 'Shut the fuck up,' a man said. 'No one is fucking dead.' Others grumbled at me, too. I don't blame them. It was difficult to believe that this was happening. I tried to calm myself and then left the stand. I had completed a perfunctory course meant to be useful in medical crises. I thought I might be able to help.

Jogging around the corner, I came round to the subway. Everything was calm. A line of policemen stood there, as if to prevent people leaving, a few supporters milled around and some were even sunbathing by the wall. Jesus, I thought, this is no time to get a tan. It was only after I passed them that I realised the sunbathers were dead.

Panicked, I turned to one of the policemen. I asked: 'How many?' He just let loose a heavy, racking sob. It was too much. I ran away from the ground as fast as I could.

Stopping at a phone, I called home and got my sister. That I was calling at this time was a big shock to her. Hearing the tone of my voice frightened her and she began to cry. She asked: 'Is it bad?' I said no. But I'd made the call. That was enough.

Then I went to the pub where we were earlier. The landlady recognised me and did not throw me out. 'How bad is it,' she asked, because *Grandstand* was reporting casualties.

'Worse than Heysel,' I said.

'How many was that?'

'Thirty-nine.'

'Are you sure?'

'I saw more than that myself.' I probably hadn't but it felt like I had. I started to cry.

'Your mates?' She gestured to where we had been sitting.

'Don't know.' Then she put four optics of whisky into a half-pint glass and gave it to me.

'I should go back to the car,' I said. She nodded.

* * *

When my brother ambled up to the car, I'd been sitting on the kerb for 40 minutes or so, wondering why the others had not arrived. Few people seemed to be leaving the stadium. The empty streets made me doubt what I'd seen. Why wasn't the ground cleared? It was as if the game was being played – except that there were no roars and groans to signify action.

In the distance, though, was the noise of sirens, constant and terrifying, building with every minute. And then, suddenly, the ground emptied. My first instinct was to hit my brother but, just as at Heysel, there were many people in the same end who had no idea of the extent of the disaster. By the time we had regrouped and were ready to set off, there were arguments about the scale of what had happened. I even began to compose myself, hoping that perhaps only one or two were dead.

The journey home was horrific. Each update on the radio added more deaths to the tally. Shortly after we drove out of Sheffield, a bulletin said 12 people had died. We were shocked into silence. The count went up as the minutes passed.

You could see the look of horror on the faces in the other cars. The line of traffic made me think that this is what an army in retreat must look like. Expressions of panic were everywhere. People jumped out of their vehicles at phone boxes and tried to call home and, finding the system overloaded and out of use, ran back to the cars with fright etched on their faces. It was impossible to think or sit still – the energy of terror made it racking to sit squeezed into the back seat.

At home we went into a pub on Walton Road and began making phone calls. I phoned Big Al's mother – he, too, had moved away for work – and reassured her that he was OK, we'd seen him after the match and he'd gone to get his train. Robert, the big Ulsterman who had been with me at Heysel, stared at me, mouth agape. I asked him: 'What's wrong.'

'When did you see Al? Before we got there?'

'No, he came back to the car with you.'

'No he didn't.'

He was right. I started to shake.

'Fuck,' he said. 'Have a drink.'

* * *

I had arranged to stay with Tony in London on the Sunday night after Hillsborough before flying into New York to visit my brother. I had booked two weeks' holiday from a job working in an estate agents for an insurance company. I never went back.

When I got to his flat, Tony did not speak for an hour. Then he asked a question: 'Have you ever felt someone's ribs breaking under your feet?'

In the months afterwards, he started losing weight rapidly. Medical tests showed no clinical reasons for the condition. The doctor asked: 'Have you had any major traumas lately.' Tony could not think of any.

'It didn't occur to me,' he said.

Back home, he relayed the conversation to his girlfriend, now his wife. She dragged him back to the surgery.

No trauma. While I was running away from Hillsborough, Tony's elbow was stuck in a man's throat and neither could move in the crush behind the goal. 'I'm choking,' the man said. Frantic, Tony tried to shift his arm. It was stuck. Then the man stopped complaining.

When the doctor found out the real reason for Tony's rapid weight loss, he explained the matter in simple terms. He was Irish and not inclined to psychobabble. 'We call it the weeping willows,' Tony remembers being told by the GP. 'You can't cry and this is how it comes out. Shit. You're weeping through your arse.'

It didn't occur to most of us that we were having nervous breakdowns in the early 1990s, but we were. A lot of us screamed in the night and woke without memories. Worse were the mornings when we could recall our nightmares. Few of us went through what Tony experienced. Even fewer came away completely unscathed. There was much emotional baggage around that table in Istanbul and the bigger the game, the heavier it weighs.

* * *

PART 5

16

You'd better hurry up

Jon Dahl Tomasson puts his penalty away and the pressure is on John Arne Riise. He is probably the best striker of the ball in the team. If he scores, only one of the two final Liverpool penalty-takers needs to be successful. It could be an almost unassailable lead. Riise is hesitant in his run-up and appears to change his mind as he hits the ball. Dida saves. He didn't blast it. Now we've given them a chance. Victory was so close. So close. Let's hope there isn't another twist.

With the ticket in my possession, I began to have sympathy with Dave. You have to check it is still nestling in your pocket every couple of minutes. It was a release to be certain of entry to the match. But there were other releases that were more pressing. All hell was breaking loose in my lower intestine and, before we set off for the stadium, a visit to the toilet was necessary. There was no waiting.

Confronted with a hole in the floor, I assessed the options. The trousers I was wearing were khaki but light enough not to risk in a splashback situation – especially with a dodgy knee. They had to come off completely. Then it took some gymnastics to accommodate the painful joint in a contorted squat. Now, safe in the knowledge that there would be no disaster, I could, er, relax.

And then the realisation hit home. There was no toilet paper. Now this was ugly.

Unhooking my trousers from the hanger on the door, I went through the pockets looking for tissues. None. I did have paper. A match ticket. That was not really an option. And money. Shit.

Then the wad of two million lire notes began to look enticing. The upside was that they were next to worthless. The downside was that they contained Ataturk's image and any Turk worth his name would tear me a new arse if I dared do the unthinkable.

But there was no way out. 'Sorry Kemel,' I whispered, 'It's just the cost of living.' And, so to speak, I wiped the slate clean.

Outside, the boys were preparing to get taxis to the ground. Yes, I agreed, we should get away from here.

I told Dave what happened. 'You'll get the cash back,' he said. 'It's a legitimate business expense.'

Ah well, off to the ground.

There was a queue for taxis and, while we were waiting, a text message arrived. Someone we knew was up at the stadium and told us that the roads were blocked already. There was urgency in the words. 'Get moving now,' the message said. 'Or you'll miss the kick-off.' It was four hours before the scheduled start of the game.

Still, we were expecting plenty of entertainment. Uefa had promised a 'Fans' Festival' outside the ground as an incentive to arrive early. We were suspicious but felt that there was no option but to head for the Ataturk.

It was a long journey made tense by the driving style of our cabbie. Like many of his colleagues, he did the opposite of what was expected by his passengers. A light turns red up ahead? A quick injection of acceleration will liven things up. Oncoming traffic? Well let's see whose nerve breaks first. It was ours.

The driver took our gasps and comments as approval and grinned wildly, accepting the praise. Thankfully, the stunt-driving session came to an end. On the minus side, that was because the traffic was backed up and we were barely outside the city centre. It looked like being a long journey.

All around us were other cabs filled with Liverpool supporters, most of whom had displayed more foresight than us. They had slabs of beer with them, merrily drinking away the journey. Foolishly, we had neglected to bring provisions.

It was a huge, creeping procession, with people hanging out of taxis, minibuses and coaches, waving flags and singing and the population of Istanbul came out to enjoy the parade. The crowd was three or four people deep in some places and children ran alongside the cars handing out cardboard fans, presumably meant to help us cool down in the early-summer heat. I suggested we pile them up to make a fire, because the temperature had been dropping all day and I was sure that there would be plenty of Scousers dressed for the tropics who could die of exposure over the next few hours. I was one of them.

More than sixty minutes into the journey, we left the built-up areas and took a brand-new road – the tarmac was still black and shiny – through a landscape that was eerily familiar. 'Wasn't that Myra Hindley with a spade back there,' someone said. Could have been, because this was moorland of the bleakest sort, with one highway running across it. And that road was blocked. People had already abandoned their vehicles and were walking. We asked the driver: 'How far?' He shrugged. The meter was running and we were being lapped by pedestrians. And they were weighed down by the 24-packs of beer they were carrying.

Al knocked on the window. The other group had ditched their taxi some half a mile back. 'It's about a mile and a half,' he said. 'You can just see it over there.' He was right. The roof of the stadium was just visible in the distance when we got out of the car.

By now there was a wholesale evacuation under way. The hard shoulders were crammed with supporters and more had scrambled over the median barrier to walk against the flow of traffic heading away from the ground. From a small hillock we looked over the scene. With the flags and banners unfurled, I was again struck by the thought that this is how a medieval army must have looked. Cows and goats scattered in their wake and the clarion call of *Ring of Fire* trilled up and down the rag-tag train. It was cold and the mud was ankle deep but we had been marching for 20 years in this direction and this was no time to stop.

A mile farther on the surrounds of the stadium became visible. We could not believe the number of people who were already there. A massive crowd was installed at the back of one end of the ground and occasionally a chant slipped through the wall of noise created by circling helicopters. Our entire allocation of 20,000 appeared to be here and yet there were untold thousands still milling around the tourist sites in the city centre when we left. How many Liverpool supporters were here? And where were the Milanese?

The full horror of the Fans' Festival dawned on us during the final half-mile of the yomp across the moors. There was a band on a stage, singing and plenty of portable toilets. And that was about it. There was no food available and certainly nothing to drink. We wandered around on the edge of the crowd and even the programmes had sold out. No refreshments, no programmes and a drunken Pete Wylie doing his Jimmy Tarbuck act on stage. Were Uefa trying to start an uprising?

'Anyone lookin' for a ticket? Fella with a spare to the left of the stage.' Wylie laughed. He was the only one that thought it was funny. Boos rang out, so he played *Ring of Fire*.

Oh, there were also some PlayStation consoles. Great. Just what a football fan wants before the Champions League final. Let's warm up with Sonic the soddin' Hedgehog.

All a supporter wants is a ticket for the match, a ground that's easy to get to, places to eat and drink and enough points of entry at the stadium so that everyone can turn up in the half-hour before kick-off and get in easily. The efforts by Uefa to introduce fell-walking, concert-going and video gaming into the simple ritual of going the match shows how out of touch the people running the game are with those who pay to watch it. By now we were cold, hungry, frustrated and angry. Frankly, it would-n't have taken much to start a riot in these conditions. And, to judge from the queues to get into the actual stadium, we might easily miss the kick-off anyway, even though there were still two hours to go.

We split up and headed towards our various gates. There was little left to be said. I nodded to Dave. 'This is it,' I said. 'Yeah,' he replied. All those years, all that abuse, all those hopes… 'See you here, after.'

The rest were all behind the goal, but I was off to the side. There seemed to be chaos around my turnstile and it was easy to see why. Many of those in Liverpool shirts were from mainland Europe, a conti-nent where the concept of the queue is unknown. A German, for exam-ple, will assume that you are standing in a line of people because you enjoy it and will walk to the front. Scandinavians make a similar assumption. To do this around freezing, underfed and muddy Scousers invites a rebuke of the harshest sort and there was plenty of this going on. It was unbelievable. It took a serious effort by the authorities to turn the happiest crowd of people in the world into a surly bunch simmering with rage, but the Turks and Uefa achieved it.

Events at the gate helped to lighten the mood. The computerised entry system was clearly predicated on the chaos theory and, after the initial dispiriting few minutes, the absurdity of the situation stumbled into the comic realm. A barcode on the ticket was supposed to trigger the turnstile. But, of course, the supporter was not trusted to do this, so a Turkish steward first took the ticket, scrutinised it for a good 30 sec-onds to make sure it was not a fake and then scanned the barcode before motioning the fan forward. At this point, the supporter walks into the barrier and is halted by an immovable object. The computerised entry system simply did not work.

So the steward examines the ticket again. This time for longer, flip-ping it over to check its reverse. Yes, it's real, so he moves it over the scanner again. The gate stays firm. They shall not pass.

Another period of reflection leaves the steward bemused. Finally, he tears off the stub in traditional style and manhandles the gate open. Each of these little vignettes took four minutes. I know. I timed the bloody thing. Seven times.

'It's not going to work, just push the turnstile and save us the grief,' I said. But the Turk was tied to the ritual. He could not break the established methods. All you could do was take a deep breath and wait. It was still early. If this was happening 10 minutes before kick-off, our boys would break the gates down – and the heads of anyone who tried to stop them.

You could see why there was no beer available: Uefa couldn't organise a piss-up in a brewery. Except, of course, for their own. Because inside the ground, in tents a mere 20 yards from the salmonella factories that were producing semi-raw kebab burgers at extortionate prices for the paying fans, were the corporate guests, eating food of the highest quality and swilling alcohol in voluminous quantities.

Some supporters in shirts lurked enviously by the entrance to the hospitality tents. Those inside, dressed for the theatre or the opera, had sneers on their faces as they surveyed the shirt-wearers. Security made things easier for the privileged by moving along the unwashed. Once in the ground, I could afford to be sanctimonious again and sneered at the whole idea of corporate entertainment.

After the great lengths that the authorities had gone to outside to keep the two sets of fans apart, there was no segregation in this area. The Milan fans were visibly shocked when they entered the stadium to see red shirts everywhere. They needn't have worried. All the ire was directed against those running the sport. The Italians were sharing our suffering.

The pitch looked beautiful but the real sights were in the stands. Red banners were everywhere. Some simply said 'Liverpool' or carried the name of a favoured pub, but others were more esoteric. Would the casual observer, for example, read the words 'The distance between insanity

and genius is measured only by success' and know immediately that this
was a Liverpool banner? The use of Shanklyisms means that our standards project something more than mere support for a team. 'The only
way to be truly successful is by collective effort' is a philosophy for life
rather than a football flag. Such phrases, invariably in white lettering on
a red background, were everywhere, spicing up the simpler 'Red Army'
type flags.

The display of banners is a phenomenon that developed in the 1990s.
When we were last in a European Cup final, flags were considered
uncool, unless they were very funny. A classic 1980s vintage banner
mocked Ron Atkinson, the Manchester United manager at the time, for
his dress sense. It simply said: 'Atkinson's long leather.' If you don't
understand it immediately, it is not worth attempting to explain it. You
never will comprehend.

Now, small groups of travelling Liverpool fans make it a point of
pride to carry their own flag. At the League Cup final against Chelsea
earlier in the season, it made for a marked contrast between the two
groups of supporters. Chelsea had their Union flags and crosses of St
George with the team name on the horizontal bar. They must have
thought for a long time before going down that route.

At the Liverpool end, the energy and imagination that had gone into
the creation of the flags showed how important the football club is to
the fans. The sense of history and belief was written down for the
Londoners to envy. It was here in Istanbul, too.

It was sad, however, to see empty seats in the ground. A significant
number of Milan's tickets had not been sold. The expense of getting to
Turkey and the vague fear of Liverpool supporters had an effect.

More galling is Uefa's habit of leaving vacant the front rows of seats
all around the pitch, so supporters and their banners do not get in the
way of the advertising boards. What other sport would leave empty the
seats most likely to be seen by the television viewer during its showpiece
event? The casual observer gets the impression that the game did not

sell out. Marketing men operate on a different logic system to the average fan.

The Milan supporters had promised a spectacular, choreographed display before the match. Just before kick-off, they did their stuff. Very nice. The Liverpool fans sang *You'll Never Walk Alone* throughout it and upstaged the Italian show with flags, scarves and banners on three sides of the ground.

Time was nearing. Suddenly it didn't feel so cold. Out came the teams. It felt like 20 years had never happened.

'They all laughed at us,

They all mocked us,

They all said our days were numbered,

But I was born to be Scouse,

Victorious are we,

So if you're gonna win the cup,

You'd better hurry up…'

But those around me didn't know the song. Or were too busy singing *Ring of Fire*.

Well, here we go…

17

The Liverpool way

KAKA MAKES IT 2-2. Next it's Smicer. This will be the final time he kicks a ball competitively in a Liverpool shirt. He's been abused, castigated, laughed at and despaired over for his entire career at Anfield. Heart rates are soaring around the stadium. Except for Smicer, who calmly slots the ball home. Now it's Shevchenko. The best striker in Europe. If he scores, the pressure will be on the final Liverpool penalty-taker. It's a poor penalty and Dudek saves. The ball rebounds to Shevchenko. Most people around me stand stock still, dreading that the striker will ram the ball into the net at the second attempt. In their nervousness, they've forgotten the rules. I haven't. I'm standing on the seat letting one gigantic, cathartic howl of victory loose into the night air. In the split-second before realisation dawns, a man in front of me, perhaps the only one in the stadium to hear my scream, turns and hugs me, hooking his arms around my thighs. He's around my age, maybe older. This stranger holds me and, while everyone else suddenly goes crazy, we do not move. After a few seconds he looks up, tears running down his face.

'Twenty years,' he sobs. A tear drops softly down on to his head. It's a tender moment. Then he lets go, punches the air and runs across the seats to the front where the players are celebrating. I never see him again.

Four hours after the match, we were in an Irish bar. From Mersey to minarets in less than a week and we celebrate success against a backdrop of shamrocks and leprechauns. This is normally the last place in Istanbul that we'd choose to visit but there is a method at work here.

After three hours standing on a cramped bus trying to get back into the city centre, we needed a drink. We were tired, emotionally drained and unable to comprehend the events of the previous night. Then Al piped up as the search for an open bar began.

'I know an Irish place.' Even before the sneers had stopped, he silenced them. 'It has Sky Sports News.'

The one thing we needed even more than a drink was to see what happened. How it happened. We were still not really sure we believed it.

There were six of us now. Ian and Stephen went straight to the airport. We sat in silence, mainly. That's about as rare as winning the European Cup.

Shock brought incoherence. Tony attempted to quantify the magnitude of what we had just seen. 'It is like the best day of your life, only better,' he said. 'The way your wedding day is supposed to be, but isn't.'

'Well your wedding didn't cause mass pain to thousands of Evertonians and Mancs,' Dave said. This was an ingredient to be relished, the sweet dusting on the Turkish delight. Rivalry brings such pleasure - and pain.

Dave had hit the jackpot. After all those years being the butt of jokes, he had seen a game, a victory, that will rank even higher than 1977, when the European Cup was won for the first time in Rome. It is the greatest night of all and he was there. Already, he was compiling lists of those who had mocked him in the past but not made the journey to Istanbul. Payback would soon follow.

Then the goals came on a big screen. As Crespo scored Milan's third, Andy Gray, the Sky commentator, said: 'That's it. Game over.' The bar erupted with a hail of invective. Gray played for Everton and is still regarded, two decades on, as the enemy.

For all the joy, there was discontent. Uefa did its best to spoil the trophy presentation and lap of honour. At a time when we should have been singing *our* songs, the public address system pumped out a deafening cacophony of pseudo-classical music, repeated versions of *You'll Never Walk Alone* so that even we had too much of it and the appalling *We Are The Champions* by Queen. All at decibel levels that would leave Ozzy Osborne pleading for earplugs. I mentioned that I did not hear *I Am A Liverpudlian* sung throughout the entire game. 'Most of them wouldn't know it.' Stevie said. This is a song some of us consider more pivotal than *You'll Never Walk Alone* – after all, no one else sings it. It's ours and it's exclusive. But it came about through something other than marketing, from something outside the control of the people who run the game. They feel safer with Queen than the authentic voice of the fans.

When Steven Gerrard hoisted the Cup in front of us, this was what we should have been singing. Instead, it was: 'No time for losers.' Some of us remained bitterly silent but most joined in with the song. The irony is that the line could be the motto of the game's authorities, who see fans like us in those terms.

At the other side of the bar, another loser seemed to have read our thoughts.

'I will tell you the story of a poor boy,

Who was sent far away from his home,' a voice began, slowly, unaccompanied, husky from overuse.

> 'To fight for his king and his country,
> And also the old folks back home.'

One by one, men around the bar joined in, each new vocal adding urgency as the pace quickened to the beat of stamped feet.

> 'So they put him in a Highland Division,
> Sent him off to a far foreign land,
> Where the flies swarm around in their thousands,

And there's nothing to see but the sand.
Now the battle it started next morning,
Under the Arabian Sun,
I remember that poor Scouser Tommy,
Was shot by an old Nazi gun.
As he lay on the battlefield dyin',
With the blood gushing out of his head,
As he lay on the battlefield dyin', dyin', dyin',
These were the last words he said:
Oh, I am a Liverpudlian,
And I come from the Spion Kop,
I like to sing,
I like to shout,
I get thrown out quite a lot
(Every week).
I support the team that's dressed in red,
It's the team that we all know,
It's the team that we call Liv-er-pool
And to glory we will go.
We've won the league, we've won the cup,
And we've been to Europe too,
And we played the Toffees for a laugh,
And left them feeling blue,
Five-nil!'

And there, we reclaimed the night.

The songs mean so much. All the shared knowledge and belief is most succinctly expressed in the chants, especially the long, convoluted epic that we sang that night. Over the years we've spent more time discussing this song than any other. Does the line about king and country endorse patriotism? Or does the next line undermine it with sly humour? Should he be in a Highland Division? Is it Arabian Sun? Well, it was probably radiant originally but Arabian is established by usage. On trains, coming back from games, we've thrashed out significance and interpretations. It means something.

At the League Cup final against Chelsea, when it reached the 'shot by an old Nazi gun' line, a young lad standing near me added the words 'up the bum'. He was nearly throttled for his disrespect and will not make such a mistake again. It enraged me. 'What are you, a Manc, an Evertonian?' I asked. 'Get down the Chelsea end, dickhead…'

I should go on to say we sang our songs until dawn. Instead, mentally shattered, we mooched off to bed after three or four drinks. Al would be on a plane to Australia before noon and we needed some sleep. The train to Bucharest would leave at 10pm and we knew there wouldn't be much chance to doze with the border crossings. Sometimes you have to wonder whether we put more effort into this football business than the players.

18

These were the last words
he said

IN FRONT OF THE Blue Mosque, a man in a Liverpool shirt is reading a newspaper. It is a copy of *The Sun*, a special edition of the paper printed in Istanbul. I can't believe it. The paper that accepted the police and Government's line that we were drunk, burst down the gates, stole from our own dead and urinated on them, too. The paper that told these lies under the headline: 'Hillsborough: The truth.'

He's also wearing a 'Justice for the 96' badge. If you hadn't just won the European Cup, something like that could spoil your day. It does anyway. We exchange bitter words. He's Scouse, too.

On Thursday, May 26, we became tourists. We met up and ate in a restaurant, looked around mosques and strolled around the covered bazaar, picking up presents for loved ones back home. But the enormity of what occurred the previous night meant we sleepwalked around Istanbul in a daze.

Apart from me and Dave, the rest needed to leave to get to the airport in late afternoon. There was some disquiet that the celebration parade at home was going to take place on this very night, so that most of those who made the journey to Turkey would miss the homecoming with the cup. It seemed another indication of the club's lack of concern for the supporters.

'Should have held it on Sunday,' Dave said, even though he had no idea where we would be by the close of the weekend.

'Can't be done. Everton have booked Sunday for their parade.' I said. We all laughed, bitterly.

Uefa had already indicated that Liverpool would not be allowed to defend the trophy because they finished outside the top four in the league. Everton finished fourth. The FA could have asked Uefa to include Liverpool in the next Champions League as winners and rele-gate Everton to the Uefa Cup but that was never going to happen. In a similar situation in 2000, the Spanish FA simply told the fourth-placed team that it was unthinkable for the winners not to defend the trophy. Real Madrid went in and Real Zaragoza had to be disappointed. Spain, however, does not have the shadow of Heysel lingering. Had any other team finished fourth, we suspected that the FA would have put Liverpool forward.

So we mocked Everton, creating an imaginary open-top bus ride where they celebrated finishing fourth by holding up four fingers. Winning a trophy – even the most important one in Europe – is a much less impressive event in their eyes.

No time for losers? Well that's not quite true. The way it looked was that Uefa and the FA had no time for winners.

There is a crazy logic at work in football, where the game is not about winning. Managers start the season by claiming that it is a success to merely avoid relegation, to be below average. What sort of business would tell its customers that the product they are buying is not compet-ing with the best in the market and that the most they can hope for is something barely adequate? What sort of business tells its customers not to expect glory but pray for survival? And then pays small fortunes to the players whose only hope is to finish above the bottom three teams in a division of 20. Some brands they are developing.

When managers complain that their supporters have expectations that are too high for thinking their teams – built at a cost of millions of pounds – could finish in the top eight of a division, they are bringing the game into disrepute. When they field weakened teams in the FA and League Cups, claiming all that matters is Premiership survival, they should be sacked.

Not every club can have the assets of Chelsea but the art of management is to use limited resources to achieve. Sport is about scaling heights, chasing glory and lifting the soul, not encouraging and rewarding mediocrity. When it stops being about glory, it starts to die.

Attendances in football are beginning to slip for the first time in more than a decade and little wonder. When a manager starts the season by saying that he will be happy with 40 points, what incentive is there to get excited about football matches?

It does not matter whether it is feasible or not, but a fan wants to start the season believing that there is an outside chance of snatching glory. A cup run, perhaps, or an unlikely tilt at promotion. To have a manager say, up front, that he is not good enough, his players are not good enough, should be grounds for dismissal.

But the reality is that the game rakes in so much money that it can be more comfortable to sit back, do the bare minimum and count the piles of cash. The cost of success – higher expectations from fans, higher wages for players – can be irksome and avoided by just muddling along. It is easier, and almost as profitable, to be average.

Football is an amazing business. A cynical owner can asset-strip a club on an annual basis and know that the customers will come back again next year, despite the treatment meted out to them. That is because fans do not see their relationship with the club as a commercial transaction. The team is woven into the supporter's being; it is part of the supporter's sense of self. And the clubs ruthlessly exploit this.

For Liverpool supporters brought up in the days of Shankly, it is even worse. The great man worked hard to create the bond between team and fans, to make the people on the terraces believe that the 11 men on the pitch were an embodiment of the supporter's hopes and aspirations.

When a policeman kicked a scarf off the pitch during a celebration, Shankly upbraided him. 'Don't you know what this means,' he said, conspicuously putting the scarf around his own neck.

Shankly's political heritage was in the south Ayrshire coalfields and he brought it to a city ready for his message. He built a side based on socialist ethics, where teamwork was paramount. And he made the supporters feel that they were part of that team.

The cynic may say he was a con-man. To us he is football's version of the holy spirit. The irony is that, with little to work with, he created a club that could easily be turned into a multimillion pound business and built a sense of loyalty among the fans that was ripe for abuse in a capitalist world. To be fair, Liverpool supporters have been less abused in the money-obsessed world of the Premiership than most. Yet when Thai despots with appalling human-rights records attempt to buy the club, as happened less than a year before the triumph in Istanbul, it is a worrying portent for the future.

It's hard to see who is carrying Shankly's flame at Anfield.

Except us. The fans. And the people in power at the club don't really want us.

* * *

Those who sneer at supporters for the way they still follow their team in the face of sometimes dreadful treatment miss one important fact: most fans know how they are being exploited. The clubs and their followers live in parallel universes. Each party takes what they want from the relationship and chooses to ignore the negative aspects of the exchange. Ironically, the man on the terraces understands the hopes and expectations of the boardroom far more clearly than the money-men comprehend what drives the fan.

Much has changed between Heysel and Ataturk. In Brussels, the overwhelming majority of Liverpool fans had Scouse accents. In Istanbul, there were not only a variety of accents, but a babble of languages in the Liverpool sections. It is the same on the pitch. In the 1980s, British and Irish players dominated. Now, who knows how many nationalities are on the team sheet?

Global appeal makes for global profits, but at what cost? In 2005, Manchester United supporters promised insurrection if Malcolm Glazer and his family took control over Old Trafford. While the American tycoon hoovered up shares with borrowed money, those fans who had rushed with glee to buy into the club when it was listed on the stock market promised to resist. They didn't. The irony of a group called Shareholders United objecting to a financial takeover no doubt made the pain of the anti-Glazer lobby more acute. Liverpool supporters enjoyed their rivals' discomfort in public and in private wondered what was so bad about the owner of the Tampa Bay Buccaneers American football team. Compared to Thaksin Shinawatra, the Prime Minister of Thailand, Glazer looked like prince charming.

When, at half-time in Istanbul, the Milan fans unfurled a banner proclaiming their support for United and their objections to the global-isation of football, it felt like they were adding insult to injury. Not only were we 3-0 down, but the Italians were giving succour to our worst enemies. It sent me into a rage.

Before the year was out, Americans would be measuring up Anfield. 'It's a great brand,' Robert Kraft, the billionaire owner of the New England Patriots, said. But it is not a brand. It is not a consumer prod-uct. The elements of love, belief and loyalty that make football clubs transcend the mere commercial and elevate the game's significance mil-itate against it being a brand. Sever the link, the emotional ties, and the clubs will become a brand, another facet of pop culture to be taken up and dropped as fashion dictates. The profiteers do not see this. They see only the short-term bottom line.

The irony is that so many of the football clubs that churn out profits and operate without recourse to anything other than financial reward grew out of Church teams. How did Liverpool and Everton, those rival siblings, end up trying to build empires in the Far East after developing from the single spilt embryo that was St Domingo's church team? What would the Wesleyans who came together to form Aston Villa think of the club today as run by 'Deadly' Doug Ellis?

The only thing that seems to have been retained from the early days of the game is the quasi-religious significance that supporters attach to the teams. 'It's like a religion for these people,' is often said, with a sneer, by those who fancy themselves above such vulgar matters as football. Yet that is exactly where many of the clubs come from.

Even when the church was not a component, the game grew from community and comradeship. The workers at the Newton Heath branch of the Lancashire and Yorkshire Railway formed a side for the sheer pleasure of playing sport with colleagues. The club they created would become that most profit-minded of institutions, Manchester United.

Churches and workers' associations, spirituality and socialism, would have appealed to Shankly. Thai politicians, American capitalists and Russian oligarchs have very different priorities when assessing the potential for profit.

The game has been globalised and it is an uncomfortable feeling for those for whom the local connection has traditionally been one of the significant factors in support. To fans from outside the city, singing of 'poor Scouser Tommies' and declaring 'I was born to be Scouse' may seem like an attempt to keep them on the outside and maintain some sort of proprietorial exclusivity. But that would be missing the point. The clubs grew out of churches and social groups and are institutions that have roots in the community where they were founded. Many of us believe that it remains important to recognise that pedigree while at the same time welcoming anyone from anywhere in the world who is committed enough to support the team.

As businesses, it is better for the clubs to shed any local baggage that restricts their audience. In my circle of friends, no one owns a replica shirt or buys memorabilia, except for their children. I suspect the club would rather replace us with people who buy kits every time they change and have a less jaundiced attitude to those in the boardroom.

'I felt like the Mancs have felt for years,' I said, explaining the few Scousers around me in the stadium by alluding to Manchester United's massive support from outside their city.

'We all want to be Barcelona,' Dave said. 'But even Barcelona don't want to be Barcelona.' Around the table in a small courtyard adjacent to the covered bazaar, everyone nodded.

It was true. The Catalan identity that turned the club into a cultural symbol limits their global appeal. They want bigger markets. Everybody wants bigger markets.

* * *

A number of years ago, I interviewed for the position of official Liverpool website editor. A rather camp young man asked me what I knew about the club as an opening gambit. 'Where do you want me to start?' I asked. 'At the beginning?' He reacted with horror. 'No, no, no. We don't want all that history stuff. Only the future matters.'

Like the guilty, marketing men hate the past. Only the old are interested in history and young is the demographic they're looking for. In football, it's even more pronounced. Every season has to be bigger and better than the one before. Competitions can be rebranded every few years so that records can be broken in each newly-named, longstanding tournament without any reference to the overall picture. So, the top flight of English football, the Premiership, only exists from 1992. Who cares about the 104 forgotten years of the Football League? Heritage and culture take too long to build so it's better to grab the floating fan, milk them for all they're worth before they move on and let the next generation of punters 'grow' themselves, because looking beyond your nose is almost as bad as looking backwards.

The game has moved from having deep-seated psychological connections with the community in which the club is based, to a pop industry where a new and different design of shirt can create a generation of fans or, better still, a good-looking superstar can put 10,000 on the gate and millions in the merchandising coffers. But, when David Beckham went from Manchester United to Real Madrid, how many of the popettes went with him? Love and loyalty, the driving forces of the traditional supporter, are not respected when it's easier and more lucrative to chase the infatuated and the feckless.

When the name on the back of the shirt becomes more important than the badge on the front, the entire essence of team sport comes into question. Stevie Gerrard failed to understand that when he refused to share the cup after the game. He needs to be generous, even when he's carrying the team.

This is not criticism of non-Scouse Liverpool fans, some of whom are far more motivated – obsessed, even – than people on Merseyside. Their energy and commitment to the cause is stunning and admirable. It's just that the club feels more comfortable with them, values them more – simply because they buy more – than the boys from the likes of the Flat Iron and the Yankee, whose flags, songs and legends are home-made.

* * *

The boys from the Flat Iron and the Yankee parted in Istanbul with rare hugs – physical contact usually only occurs briefly after goals have been scored. This momentous trip had joined the litany of shared experiences – good and bad – that bind us together. New friends are great, but there is something deeper, more satisfying, about being with people who have retained a mutual closeness over the decades. Football may even learn that lesson one day.

But that was it. You could spend a lifetime in Istanbul and never truly say you know the place, but one long afternoon as tourists was enough for us. We didn't come for the sights and the city had little use for us now the game was over. Maybe one day we'd come back and see it properly. It could never match these few days, though.

Back at the hotel, we packed for the journey. Clean clothes were no longer an option. We'd planned the trip up until kick-off. After that moment, life could take care of itself.

As we left, someone was still giving voice to *Ring of Fire*. 'Easier to learn than *Scouser Tommy*,' Dave said. He was right. But whenever we hear it from now on, it will recall Istanbul. It is a happy sound.

'Enjoy that?'

Dave smirked. 'There'd have to be something wrong with you not to come to this. Wait until I see the people who didn't bother and watched on telly. The abuse they'll get…'

We boarded the train and hung out of the window as we pulled away. One last look at Istanbul and then to our reeking beds.

God's Scouse, we were feeling good and tonight, at least, there would be no nightmares.

Epilogue

O VER A RAPTUROUS SUMMER, Uefa relented, allowed Liverpool to defend their trophy and the future looked bright. But fate had one last trick to remind everyone that there are no happy endings. The Champions League draw placed Anderlecht in the same group as the holders. This meant, that on October 19, 2005, Liverpool would be back in Brussels for the first time, 20 years on.

Liverpool won the game 1-0. There was no trouble.

And no official delegation from Liverpool Football Club made the two-mile detour to lay a wreath at the plaque for the dead of Heysel.

In memory of those who have never been given justice

Rocco Acerra, John Alfred Anderson, Colin Mark Ashcroft, James Gary Aspinall, Bruno Balli, Kester Roger Marcus Ball, Gerard Bernard Patrick Baron, Simon Bell, Barry Sidney Bennett, David John Benson, David William Birtle, Tony Bland, Alfons Bos, Paul David Brady, Andrew Mark Brookes, Carl Brown, David Steven Brown, Giancarlo Bruschera, Henry Thomas Burke, Peter Andrew Burkett, Andrea Casula, Giovanni Casula, Paul William Carlile, Nina Cerullo, Raymond Thomas Chapman, Willy Chielens, Gary Christopher Church, Joseph Clark, Paul Clark, Gary Collins, Giuseppina Conti, Stephen Paul Copoc, Tracey Elizabeth Cox, Dirk Daeninckx, James Philip Delaney, Christopher Barry Devonside, Christopher Edwards, Dionisio Fabbro, Vincent Michael Fitzsimmons, Thomas Steven Fox, Jacques Francois, Eugenio Gagliano, Francesco Galli, Jon-Paul Gilhooley, Barry Glover, Ian Thomas Glover, Derrick George Godwin, Giancarlo Gonnelli,

Alberto Guarini, Roy Harry Hamilton, Philip Hammond, Eric Hankin, Gary Harrison, Stephen Francis Harrison, Peter Andrew Harrison, David Hawley, James Robert Hennessy, Paul Anthony Hewitson, Carl Darren Hewitt, Nicholas Michael Hewitt, Sarah Louise Hicks, Victoria Jane Hicks, Gordon Rodney Horn, Arthur Horrocks, Thomas Howard, Thomas Anthony Howard, Eric George Hughes, Alan Johnston, Christine Anne Jones, Gary Philip Jones, Richard Jones, Nicholas Peter Joynes, Anthony Peter Kelly, Michael David Kelly, Giovacchino Landini, Carl David Lewis, Roberto Lorentini, Barbara Lusci, Franco Martelli, Loris Messore, Gianni Mastroiaco, David William Mather, Brian Christopher Mathews, Sergio Mazzino, Francis Joseph McAllister, John McBrien, Marion Hazel McCabe, Joseph Daniel McCarthy, Peter McDonnell, Alan McGlone, Keith McGrath, Paul Brian Murray, Lee Nicol, Stephen Francis O'Neill, Jonathon Owens, Luciano Papaluca, William Roy Pemberton, Luigi Pidone, Benito Pistolato, Patrick Radcliffe, Domenico Ragazzi, Antonio Ragnanese, Carl William Rimmer, David George Rimmer, Claude Robert, Graham John Roberts, Steven Joseph Robinson, Henry Charles Rogers, Mario Ronchi, Domenico Russo, Tarcisio Salvi, Gianfranco Sarto, Colin Andrew Hugh William Sefton, Inger Shah, Paula Ann Smith, Mario Spanu, Adam Edward Spearritt, Giuseppe Spolaore, Philip John Steele, David Leonard Thomas, Patrik John Thompson, Peter Reuben Thompson, Stuart Paul William Thompson, Peter Francis Tootle, Christopher James Traynor, Martin Kevin Traynor, Kevin Tyrrell, Tarcisio Venturin, Colin Wafer, Jean-Michel Walla, Ian David Whelan, Martin Kenneth Wild, Kevin Daniel Williams, Graham John Wright, Claudio Zavaroni